The strategies presented in this book are based on the experience of the author. If you make your own investments, the author and publisher strongly suggest you utilize the services of a professional in the fields of law, real estate, and finance. The author and publisher disclaim any responsibility for any liability, loss, or risk, personal or otherwise, which is incurred as a consequence, directly or indirectly, of the use and application of any of the contents of this book.

Contents

PART I
Lessons From the Rich

PART II
SIX SIGMA

PART III
Investing in Real Estate

This book is dedicated to my wife.
Thank you for all your support and understanding.
I love you.

Special thanks to my parents, brother, and in-laws
for all your guidance throughout my life.

<u>Introduction</u>

Have you ever wondered what the wealthy and successful people are doing to make it to the pinnacle of society? Have you ever contemplated why someone else is a CEO and you are not? Have you ever thought, "What are they doing right that I am not?" The truth is there's nothing magical about being successful. You just have to be committed to learning from those around you that are successful. The difficult thing is not everyone has a personal mentor they can call on during the middle of the workday to get counseling on how to build wealth. This book takes years of my experiences, my learning, and the mentorship I have received from financially successful individuals and presents it in an easily digestible format that is candid and to the point. The book is segmented into three basic categories: wealth building lessons, real estate tactics, and utilizing Six Sigma. In this book I share with you not only the basic foundation of how hundreds of my acquaintances have become wealthy and now lead successful lives, but I also give specific examples of what those successful people did to vastly increase their wealth.

I assume that since you picked up this book you have an interest in increasing your wealth. My intent is not to write a Pulitzer Prize winning novel, but to inform you of the lessons I have observed from wealthy individuals I have known through the years. I wrote this book to share the unique experiences and relationships I've had with wealthy business owners, business managers, and leaders around the world. From these relationships, I have been able to gain quite a bit of knowledge and understanding of what made these people successful. I have gained this information from four main sources. In no particular order, they are: leaders I worked with as an officer in the U.S. Army, business owners I audited while working with GE Capital, clients I worked with as the owner of a real estate brokerage firm, and relationships with various business leaders I have developed over the course of my lifetime. This information is the result of

25+ years of listening to those successful influencers around me and learning both from their mistakes as well as their success.

Let me start by sharing a little information about my background and experiences. From the Army I gained a tremendous amount of leadership experience and logistics management experience. The Army is broken down into two basic categories, the fighters and those that support the fighters. I love the way the Army developed me. They placed me in a program where they made me a fighter (a tank platoon leader). A few years later, they moved me to a variety of logistics roles where I supported the fighters. This program provides the logisticians with first hand experience of what it's like to try and fight without the parts, fuel, food, or ammunition you desperately need. When I tell people I was in the Army, I sometimes get a face with a wrinkled up nose staring back at me. This usually comes from people who have no experience with the military. Many people assume that everyone in the military is uneducated or was forced to join in lieu of going to prison. On the contrary, I frequently worked side by side with Princeton and Harvard MBAs, United States Military Academy graduates, and several officers that went on to become senior executives at fortune 500 companies.

After seven years with the Army, I was recruited by GE Capital to join their Six Sigma Black Belt program. This was in essence an internal consulting job where I led teams to drive out defects in processes by utilizing leadership and a statistically based methodology called Six Sigma. At the time Jack Welsh was the long running CEO of GE and he embraced Six Sigma with a passion. I was a believer in Six Sigma and an even bigger believer in Jack Welsh. He was passionate. He was inspiring. He challenged the status quo. He challenged management to constantly improve, refine and squeeze more productivity out of his business units. At the time GE was considered to have one of the most talented management teams in the world. Learning from the leaders and managers I interacted with on a daily basis was fascinating! The company would not allow us to remain stagnant. We were always pushing to improve our processes and squeeze productivity out of our business.

After my tenure as a Black Belt I was promoted to the senior leadership team and placed in charge of quality and training. I later moved to Florida and took a position within GE Capital on their audit team. The Six Sigma experience helped me understand how everything can be broken down into a process. The beauty of Six Sigma is that it can be applied to any business and the benefits are practically unlimited. I will delve deeper into Six Sigma later. The financial management experience at GE has also been invaluable to me in my career. Finally, the auditing experience was incredible. I was actually being paid to probe businesses. Due to the nature of the circumstances, I was usually sent to audit high producing companies with millions of dollars of exposure or low producing companies that were on the verge of bankruptcy. I had a microscope to view what the strong companies were doing right and what the weak companies were doing wrong. As someone who wanted to open up my own business, I was salivating at this incredible opportunity!

After a few years of soaking up information as an auditor, I couldn't wait to start my own business. I decided to pursue something that I was always passionate about, real estate. I had invested in commercial and residential real estate for over a decade and thought it would be a great field to transition into. After a few years of learning the business with a national firm, I hung out a shingle as quickly as I could and opened my own real estate brokerage firm. It was a boutique firm, but in a high end area. Most of the clients I worked with were wealthy, and yet again I found myself in a field where I could soak up knowledge from hundreds of financially successful people.

I want to stress a statement I made in a previous paragraph, "Listening to those successful influencers around me and learning both from their mistakes as well as their success." The willingness to *listen* and *learn* is one trait that sets me apart from my peers. I've known plenty of people that get to interact with millionaires. I've also known plenty of people that interact with millionaires that *want* to learn from them. However, most of these people don't actually listen and learn. Their problem is their cup is already full. They go into a situation thinking, "I'm more educated or I'm more intelligent than this wealthy person. Why should I listen to what they have to say?" I've seen plenty of people half-heartedly listen to wealthy individuals, only to focus on the negative and not focus on actually learning from them. This is why so many people *fail* to be successful. They get so entrenched in their ways; they will not consider or accept any other person's ways. Whether it is stubbornness, ignorance, arrogance or fear of change, the end result is the same. They are not capable of changing their ways, and therefore are unable to really maximize their potential and become financially successful.

As an example, several years ago I was conducting an audit. The business owner had run a tremendously successful business for two decades or more. Unfortunately his company's bottom line was shrinking and had been for the last few years. I had a specific set of guidelines to follow for the audit and did so very efficiently. However, I viewed this as an opportunity to gain knowledge from a very successful business owner. This particular situation was intriguing because I also had an opportunity to see how a very successful person could make mistakes and let a company start to slide. I viewed this as a tremendous learning opportunity. There was another auditor there who also had a specific set of guidelines to follow for the audit and he also performed his job very efficiently. The difference between the two of us became apparent during our interviews with the owner. The other auditor would talk over him, and behaved in a borderline arrogant manner. His cup was full. He was not there to learn and understand. Unlike my counterpart, I tried my best to take advantage a great opportunity and picked the brain of business owner. I complemented him on his ability to run a successful business for so long. I was polite and listened to his complaints. I asked probing questions about the business operations. I went in with an empty glass and hoped he could fill it up with knowledge. I watched the way he managed and interacted with his employees. I watched the way he engrossed himself in servant leadership, a style of leadership in which the leader focuses a large amount of effort in assisting those employees that report to him. Among other things, I learned the reason for the downturn in sales was due to a market change. He was an owner of multiple ACE Hardware stores which sold a myriad of products, but these particular stores relied heavily on selling room air conditioners, also known as window units. The customers that he sold the most volume to were hotels. As the hotels in the region transitioned from room air conditioners to central air conditioning the room air conditioner market quickly disappeared.

My counterpart and I both conducted our audits successfully. My counterpart probably left feeling a bit superior and went back to his office hoping to get a promotion within the next five years or so. I went back to my office with another option. I went back with my cup filled with the knowledge of a successful business owner. I was able to glean quite a bit of insight from a pro in the retail business. I learned from his leadership style and I learned from his mistakes in market strategy. I made one more small deposit into my bank account of business knowledge. I knew that each deposit I made would give me one more opportunity to be financially successful in the future.

You could say that my personality has enabled me to absorb the knowledge of my clients and those other influencers around me throughout my lifetime. I am motivated by money. I don't let it control me and I'm not obsessed with it, but I do tend to focus my "working" time trying to make more of it. I'm always looking for ways to make more money and doing it with the least amount of effort. This is another reason I listen and learn from those wealthy individuals I encounter. I did not have the luxury of inheriting a fortune. I am not gifted in any artistic or athletic way that enables me to earn millions in the sports or entertainment industry. I was fortunate enough to grow up in a caring middle class family. I classify myself as a "grinder." By grinder, I mean I stick my nose to the grindstone and pound out success. I learned at an early age that success is not something handed to you on a plate. You have to earn it. I also learned as a young adult to understand myself and accept my limitations. By accepting them I don't mean I allow them to define me or slow me down. I mean I study my strengths and weaknesses and come up with a plan to succeed by putting me in a situation to best utilize my strengths. As an example, I learned from several of my mentors at an early age that obtaining a college education was not a requirement for becoming financially successful. I did, however, learn that it greatly increased your chances of becoming financially successful. Sure, every once in a while you come across those kids like Bill Gates that drop out of Harvard because they need to get on with their startup companies like Microsoft. I, on the other hand, understood that I did not fall into the Bill Gates category and needed others to teach me about managing money and running a business. I knew I did not have the mental ability or high school grades to win an academic scholarship to college. With this in mind, I looked for another way to get a scholarship. I found a fantastic alternative, an Army Reserve Officer Training Corps (ROTC) scholarship. This not only paid for the majority of my tuition and expenses in college, but it also gave me something equally as important, leadership experience. Not only did I receive years of leadership experience as an Army cadet in ROTC, but I also earned a commission as an officer in the U.S. Army upon graduation. This led to seven years of honing my leadership skills and learning from some of the best leaders you could imagine. By the end of my tenure as an officer in the Army, I was recognized by U.S. Army Personnel

Command as being in the top 10% of all of my peers and as a reward I was awarded a position teaching military leadership at the University of Houston.

Later in life, I understood that earning a Masters in Business Administration would help me increase my chances of becoming financially successful. In the late 1990's I was already successful. I had a fantastic career with GE and was earning more than practically everyone else I knew in my age group. I looked up to my mentors that were company officers at GE. Their salaries without stock options and benefits went deep into the six figure range. Each one of my successful mentors at GE had an MBA. That was a strong enough correlation for me! But why pay for it if I don't have to? I found out that GE would pay for my graduate classes at the University of Iowa as long as I made a B or higher in the course. You can bet I did everything I could to make sure I did not have to pay for those classes! I had so many friends that laughed at me. They made good incomes and thought I was cheap for not spending a few thousand per semester on tuition. These were the friends that would refuse to use coupons because they thought it was "beneath" them. They had to stay in the five star hotels instead of the more basic ones. Why? The answer is simple. Vanity. It's a sad reality, and it's one that costs many people lots of money in the long run. Why not use grocery coupons? Why not stay in clean, lower end hotels? Better yet, why not stay in high end resorts and pay the lower price usually only the low end hotels offer? Yes, I am frugal. Why? Because the financially successful mentors I've had over the years taught me to be frugal. Frugality is one of the lessons I can share with you as we go through the lessons of the wealthy. Let's get started!

PART I
Lessons From the Rich

Leadership Vs. Management

I use the terms leadership and management frequently throughout this book. I want to take a moment to differentiate the two. While they are often intertwined and the terms are frequently used interchangeably, there is a distinct difference.

I always preferred the Army's definition of leadership, the art of influencing soldiers to accomplish the mission. Exchange the word soldier with employee and this definition can be applied to any organization in the world. The reason I prefer this definition is because of the word art. Leadership truly is an art form. It is not a gift. It is not something inherited, or something you are born with. I always laugh when I hear the term "born leader." Leadership is like any other art, craft, or skill. It can be taught, practiced, honed and refined.

When I taught military leadership at the University of Houston, I used the U. S. Army's doctrine for leadership training. It segmented the art of leadership into thirteen distinct dimensions. These dimensions consisted of skills such as influence, initiative, tack and judgment. Each of these dimensions could be honed and refined as well. Several people have come to me over the years and said, "I can't lead that many people," or "I'm just not cut out to be a leader," or "I'm too nervous to get in front of those people and take charge." My response is always the same. I tell them to study and learn leadership skills, then go out and practice. For someone who has little or no leadership experience, the easiest way to practice is by taking leadership roles in volunteer groups. These can be at the office, in your neighborhood community, in your religious community or practically anywhere. I always recommend taking baby steps and starting with small groups at first, then building your way up. People often say, "Taking a leadership role in a volunteer group is one thing, but leading people at work is completely different." I agree. It is completely different. It's typically easier to lead a group of individuals at work that report to you as opposed to leading a group of your peers in a volunteer group. Leading peers is one of the toughest leadership challenges because you really have to get creative to find ways to influence people that don't work for you. They can walk away at the drop of a hat. When it comes to improving your leadership skills, all it takes is practice.

Leadership is a skill that must be constantly honed. Like any skill, if you don't use it you will get rusty. Stay active in your leadership roles, no matter how minute they may be. I could always tell a distinct difference at GE between the leaders that had been "individual managers" or managers that didn't manage any subordinates, vs. the managers of large numbers of personnel. The individual managers often lost touch with the employees, as they did not have to interact often with the masses. They often became more removed or unforgiving, and with less compassion thus became less effective leaders.

Energy and enthusiasm are contagious, and most great leaders have these qualities. Once you exhibit these qualities, they naturally ooze out and have a habit of sticking to those around you. I was with my wife and some friends in Planet Hollywood one evening waiting for a table. We went upstairs and waited in a logjam of several other people also waiting for a table. As the hostess tried to direct each party to their respective table, I noticed several people around me were craning their necks, looking at someone off to the side. I was curious and peered around the corner to see what everyone else was looking at. At first, I just noticed a dirty table and a busboy cleaning. I couldn't see what had mesmerized so many people. I was about to give up searching when I noticed that everyone was staring at the busboy! He was putting all the dishes into his plastic pan at the speed of mach 1. It only took him seconds to bus each table and move to the next. He wasn't just quick at putting away dishes. You could tell he was making a concerted effort to make his job enjoyable. Through his energy and enthusiasm, he transformed a dirty and mundane job into an exciting spectacle that everyone wanted to watch! While at GE Capital, the company was consistently focused on the idea of being energized. I still have a laminated card the company handed out to the management staff. It had the company values listed on the card that it expected to see from each person on the management staff across the company. One of those values was to constantly demonstrate personal energy "with infectious enthusiasm." I think about the influence that busboy had over so many strangers just by sharing some of his infections enthusiasm. It's no surprise that some of the best leaders show their enthusiasm and let others feed off of it. We all have the power within us to be energetic. We just have to let it out.

Leadership is, in its best form, inspirational. Pulitzer Prize winner James Macgregor Burns writes in his book, Leadership, that transformational leadership allows both leaders and their subordinates to attain higher levels of motivation and morality. This inspirational leadership is the pinnacle of what great leaders strive for. Think about Presidents and great political leaders that have inspired others to work for and support them for years at a time. Think about leaders in war that ask volunteers to engage in life threatening missions. Sir Winston Churchill, Adolph Hitler, and Harry S. Truman each inspired masses of people to support their country. Japanese fighter pilots in WWII were inspired to give the ultimate sacrifice for their country. The power of inspirational leadership is an awesome force.

Impactful leaders are able to visualize the process and what it takes to succeed in their own minds. More importantly, they are able to communicate this vision to their peers and subordinates. Some of the best leaders I've met just did the simple things right. I remember a young Captain giving an operations order to his subordinates about an upcoming mission in the desert. He pulled out a cardboard box and drew out how he envisioned the battle was going to unfold. Everyone there knew exactly what to do and when just because of the way he designed and delivered his vision. Another instance I will always remember was a Colonel in charge of a brigade. He had the most simple and yet effective way of conducting a preparation prior to a battle. He held a brigade level walk through of his operations order. He brought in every officer in his brigade, well over one hundred of us, for a walk-through. This was conducted in an enormous sandbox which was created as a scaled down model of the terrain we would be covering. As we literally walked through the terrain model, he made each of us mimic the sound of our weapons and aircraft so each unit could understand what the other units were doing as we moved through the mission. He made the helicopter pilots literally hold out their arms and make a *wop-wop-wop* sound. The tankers made a *grrrrrrrrrrrr* sound. It seemed outrageous at first, but everyone understood where their friendly units were and how they were all going to work together in concert. Another impactful leader I had was a young executive at GE Capital named Larry. He would walk around and mentor each of his managers constantly. When he would grab them in the hallway, he would either hash out his ideas on paper right there or rush them over to the nearest white board and passionately draw out his ideas and visions. Leaders who can strategically envision the end state through whatever means necessary are the leaders who are going to make an impact in their organization. These are the leaders that can truly change an organization. We often see managers that are flash in a pan. They make a big splash initially but no sustainable systems develop. When weak leaders leave an organization they often leave their teams in disarray because no systems, backbone, or infrastructure has been developed. Impactful, strategic leaders can develop processes and systems to ensure success. A sign of an impactful leader is after she leaves, the subordinate leadership team doesn't miss a beat.

Leadership is passionate and drives subordinates to a common goal or vision. The leader determines the vision, goals and objectives for the company while the manager ensures the employees meet those goals and objectives. Among other things, management entails watching over subordinates, counseling them on their ability or lack thereof to produce to pre-determined metrics, and keeping them focused on their objectives. All great leaders are great managers. Not all great managers are great leaders.

Wealthy, Financially Successful, and Rich

I intermix the terms financially successful, wealthy, and rich throughout this book. Robert Kiyosaki, author of Rich Dad Poor Dad, wrote about how lucky we are to live in the United States and that alone should be considered a wealthy lifestyle. I absolutely agree. There are a handful of countries on this planet that offer the security and resources necessary for anyone to live a long, healthy life. We should be grateful to have the privilege of living in a rich country. I did not fully understand this concept until I went overseas and worked in third world countries. I learned that all the things I had so easily taken for granted such as freedom of speech, freedom of religion, running water, and health care are not rights. They are privileges. If you are lucky enough to live in one of these wealthy countries, then consider yourself rich!

This book, however, does not tackle global social reform. When I write about the wealthy, the rich, and the financially successful,

I am writing about individuals that have demonstrated financial success within our wealthy country and have a net worth at least in the $1,000,000 range. Many of the people I write about have a net worth in the $10,000,000 range and I even write about one billionaire!

Lessons

As I mentioned in the introduction, the lessons I'm writing about come from my personal experiences from leaders I worked with as an officer in the U.S. Army, business owners I audited while working with GE Capital, clients I worked with as the owner of a real estate brokerage firm, and relationships with various business leaders over the last 25+ years. I have worked with and studied under hundreds of millionaires during this time and I was even fortunate enough to study under one billionaire.

Finding Hidden Value

At first I thought so many of my wealthy acquaintances were just lucky when it came to finding a great financial opportunity. I likened it to winning the lotto. I thought, "Man if only I could have that sort of luck, I could be rich too!" I thought they were just "falling" into these great deals and finding out later what a goldmine they had purchased. I was wrong. Over the years I noticed that these people kept "falling" into great deals over and over. They kept finding those diamonds in the rough that didn't look like much on the surface, but once polished turned out to be worth a fortune.

Many of my clients who invested in real estate had this talent. They could find a residential or commercial property and look past the defects. They would make low offers when purchasing to further reduce the risk. They would not get caught up in any sort of emotional attachment to the property. They would assess the potential value of the property, make an offer well below that value, and move on to the next project if the offer was not accepted. There was no emotional mourning over the deal that got away. It was strictly business.

A friend of mine, Brett, owned a resort in south Florida. Brett went to college and received a good education in hotel and restaurant management. Upon graduating he landed an entry level management job with a large national hotel chain. He could have followed the path of all the other junior managers and worked his way through middle management, possibly upper management, and then retired. For many people out there, this is the path that's expected. It's the safe path that we've been taught. My friend decided to take another path. He found some real estate investors looking for a resort property to purchase in south Florida. He convinced them that he could manage the property at a relatively low salary, but he wanted a share in ownership of the company. Most people would look for a higher salary, but not him. He understood the real value in this long-term relationship was owning a piece of the pie. He wanted to earn some "sweat equity" from the company. The partners agreed to his request and they eventually purchased a resort. The time period was in the mid 1990s. He and his partners were able to see that the value was not in running the resort, but in selling them as condos. This was long before the real estate boom which peaked in 2005-2006. They weren't following the condo craze. They were pioneers leading the way.

This successful transaction led to a larger investment in northeast Florida. My friend, along with the same group of investors, purchased a Radisson hotel that was on the waterfront in the downtown Jacksonville area. There was plenty of value in the brick and mortar, that is the building itself, but there was also tremendous value in the land. When they purchased the hotel, they also obtained a large amount of waterfront real estate that was unutilized. With Jacksonville hosting an upcoming NFL Super Bowl they understood they would be able to charge vendors a premium for the space. They also understood the value of a brand. They rebranded the hotel under the Wyndham name and are now able to increase prices for a room. They constantly look for opportunities to unlock and utilize the hidden value they have. They took an underutilized parking lot and now rent out parking spaces for entertainment events. They looked at an ugly unused rooftop and realized it had a great view of the river and city skyline. They turned it into a beautiful deck and now rent it out for parties and events. He was able to see beyond the obvious and look at the potential value the property had to offer, and it has worked out magnificently for him.

While obtaining my MBA from the University of Iowa, I met an incredibly successful entrepreneur named Ed Moldt. Ed was a professor of mine. At the time he was a billionaire who owned upwards of 200 businesses. I hung on every word he uttered. He has an incredible life story in which he made a fortune, lost it, and then built an empire from the ground up. I'll tell more about his rise and fall as a billionaire later. For now I'll tell about his ability to find hidden value.

One evening in class Ed taught us about squeezing value out of an investment. He shared a story with us about running into a friend of his having breakfast at a restaurant in Boston one morning. His friend wanted to sell his parking garage in the Beacon Hill area, one of the higher priced real estate markets in the city. Ed asked some basic financial questions about the property and had to crunch numbers on his coffee napkin. He knew the property would go quickly and the window on this opportunity would shut quickly. He agreed on a handshake and later purchased the property. Once he took ownership of the structure, he went through the operation and found ways to increase productivity and profitability. He replaced the incumbent manager with a staff member he trusted. This resulted in more cash making its way to the bank. Apparently some cash was previously getting lost in the process of being transferred to the bank. He evaluated the layout of the parking spots and reconfigured them to allow a higher volume of cars. Instead of viewing the property only as a parking garage, he also viewed it as a potential housing development. He found the hidden value in the property and made the best use of it. He also purchased the property for its potential instead of just its current use to store automobiles.

Invest in Yourself

The majority of wealthy people I've met come from families with income levels in the middle or lower class. They had to start off by building up a base of funds, and then invest it wisely to really start accumulating wealth. At the same time, they had to manage their expenses in order to stay on track to becoming financially successful. They used these base jobs as a means to get started. They often used the money they saved to invest in themselves, allowing them to increase their earning power and build their wealth at a quicker pace.

Throughout this book I mention several success stories about people who have a college education. It's not a prerequisite for financial success, but it certainly increases your chances. When I say they invest in themselves, I'm not only talking about a formal four year college education. They do things like learning a valuable skill or trade. They start their own business. They invest in real estate. When you mention the word investment, most people think of the stock market. While many wealthy people do invest in the stock market, it's not the only place they invest their money.

The vast majority of millionaires I've met have at least a four year college education. Several have an advanced degree. Having the degree doesn't entitle you to wealth. It does, however, make you more attractive in the job market. Some jobs require a candidate have an advanced degree just to apply. A college education cannot guarantee you a high net worth, but it certainly can help position you for a higher paying job. The rest is up to you.

Many people earn good incomes without the benefit of a college degree. Just a few lucrative careers that do not require a four year degree include real estate salesperson, real estate broker, stockbroker, air traffic controller, commercial pilot, loan officer and financial sales. I remember when I was teaching military leadership at the University of Houston I once was looking along the wall at several photos of our financial supporters that donated the most money to the our department within the university. These people were all wealthy individuals that donated upwards of tens of thousands of dollars each. As I looked, I found the usual suspects. It was comprised mainly of retired military generals, with a smattering of Fortune 500 executives. I stopped when I noticed a photo that stood out. It was a photo of a relatively lower ranking non-commissioned officer. The pay rate between this person and the generals was enormous. "How did he get his photo on the high roller's wall?" I asked. Most non-commissioned officers don't have a college degree. I had to know his secret, so I tracked this man down. His name was Ed Farris. I found out he made his fortune selling commercial real estate. He also happened to serve in the Army Reserve as a non-commissioned officer. He was patriotic and wanted to serve his country, even though he didn't need the pay anymore. He did something more important than obtain a college degree. He invested in himself. He understood to achieve his financial dreams he would need to do something other than serve as a non-commissioned officer in the Army. He made use of the GI Bill and took some finance classes in college, but only the critical ones he needed to better understand the financing aspect of commercial real estate. He used the money he saved from his Army pay to invest in his career as a commercial real estate agent.

I have an acquaintance that is a bank manager. While he is very good at managing banks and makes a good income from doing this, he really builds his net worth by investing in real estate. Between him and his wife, they own well over 100 residential income producing properties. He has found a niche where he buys, sells and rents townhomes in a certain area of town. He knows the area so well he usually catches the distressed townhomes before they go on the market for sale. He sometimes is able to buy these at prices as low as 50% of their market value. He generally purchases properties that require minimal repairs. This way he can get them rented quickly and they can start earning income for him. He hires someone else to manage the properties. This way he is still able to continue earning an income as a bank manager. He just spends his weekends and evenings investing in real estate, and is able to significantly increase his income level. Another great thing about his situation is the fact that his income streams are diversified. Diversification reduces risk. If the rental market dips, he still has the traditional income from the bank. Conversely, if he ever gets laid off from the bank, he has the rental income to support him. By investing in his own business he created his own avenue of becoming financially successful without jeopardizing his original career.

One of the best managed businesses I audited was in California. Years prior to me auditing the business, the owners were looking for an exit strategy and one of the internal managers came up with a plan to buy out the business. The manager knew the processes, the employees, he had the necessary experience, and was a natural fit. He was able to come up with an agreeable buyout scenario and was on his way! According to my predecessors, he did a better job of running the operation than the previous owners!

Many successful people choose to invest in themselves by building their own business in lieu of working for someone else. Whether it was by choice or out of necessity, a large amount of the financially successful people I know chose to build their own business. Some of them have a "one man operation" and some have hundreds of employees. While there are pros and cons for each of these career paths, the great thing about building a business is you can build equity in the company. If you choose to work for someone else, when you stop working the pay stops. A successful business owner can build an enormous amount of equity in a company and sell it when she stops working. That's the advantage of investing in your own company instead of investing in your boss's company.

Frugality

"The top line is important, but the bottom line is more important."

Frugality is one of the most critical lessons to learn from the wealthy. It is without a doubt the easiest to learn, but it is often the most difficult to adhere to. It applies to every income bracket, every business, and every person. If you aren't careful with your money, you will find a way to lose it. This is a difficult lesson for anyone to follow. It's fun to spend money.

High paying jobs do not necessarily equate to a high net worth. Many people with great degrees and high paying jobs also acquire a lot of debt and wind up just working as a slave to their own possessions. They acquire the large house, the boat, the fancy cars, and find themselves constantly working, always wondering why they can never make enough. I've seen countless

CPAs make an income in the $60,000 - $100,000 range, but retire wealthy at an early age. They understood how to wisely invest their money and understood that it's not necessarily the top line that's important, but the bottom line. In other words, earning a high gross income is only part of the equation. Managing your debt is equally important. If you spend as much as or more than you make, it doesn't matter how high your income bracket is. You're doomed for financial failure.

I once audited a business in south Florida. At one point in time they really dominated the regional market. The owner had worked hard over the years and built up this multi-million dollar business with storefronts covering several different counties. He had created jobs for his three children, who held various positions within the family business. He wasn't extravagant in his lifestyle and didn't pay the children excessive salaries. The owner was careful with his money and very responsible about reinvesting funds back into the business. One day the owner passed away and his children inherited the company. They were always accustomed to success and a comfortable lifestyle. Unlike their father, they were not frugal and burned through the money at a rapid pace. They bought expensive cars. They often chose to hold meetings at the golf course instead of working at the storefront. They burned through millions in a short amount of time. Within a few years of the owner passing away the company was in dire straights. The father spent most of his lifetime building up this business and in a fraction of that time the children dragged it to the brink of failure. They had to look for an outside investor to purchase a controlling interest in the company in order to keep it afloat. Frugality was just not one of the children's traits, and it cost them control of the company.

I have a friend, Jimmy Sheffield, who started down the traditional path most people migrate towards. He went to college and earned a degree in accounting then passed the CPA exam. He landed a desirable position with a large accounting firm and quickly realized there was more opportunity out there for him beyond the desk job he held.

He was frugal with his money and literally saved every other paycheck. He quickly had accumulated enough for a down payment on a gas station/convenience store. He had no real experience running this type of business, but partnered with a friend that did. He was able to leverage the knowledge of an expert in the industry and learn from his friend while operating a successful business. All the while, he kept his penny-wise ways and amassed enough savings to purchase another store, this time without a partner. Soon afterwards he bought another, and another, and another. He soon became popular with the oil companies and was offered opportunities to open new stores instead of buying existing ones. He quickly became one of the largest convenience store owners in the area and was named businessperson of the year. His frugality allowed him to grow his business quickly. Success bred more success and he quickly became one of the dominant owners in the local market.

I personally struggle with frugality. I can go years living frugally, and then I tend to slip and splurge for a few years, buying luxury items. My frugality pendulum swings back and forth. I find it easier to be frugal once I've been doing it for a while and have some momentum. With me, everything seems relative. When I'm "in the zone" and have been frugal for a few years, that cruise ship vacation for $40/night in the small cabin with no windows seems pretty fantastic! Fast forward a few years and let the frugality pendulum swing the other way. Then I'll find myself complaining about the service at the all inclusive resort charging $500/night. My parents taught me the importance of being frugal. Both of my parents endured humble upbringings. My father came from a tobacco farm. As a child, his family wasn't so poverty-stricken that they could not put food on the table, but they were hungry enough to cook up the family pet duck for dinner. Although my parents did not live a life of poverty, they brushed up against that lifestyle frequently enough to understand they did not want to cross over that line. They saved as much money as possible and invested it into my father's education. Before long, he had a master's degree in finance and was teaching at Memphis State University. Even after they amassed a small fortune, they were frugal with their spending habits. They were open about the lifestyle they chose to live. They squeezed as much mileage out of their cars as they could. They chose to live in homes that were priced well within their means. They focused on savings rather than spending. They could have easily paid my entire way at the private undergraduate school I attended, but instead pushed me to find a scholarship. All the little things they did to save money helped them build up a pool of investment savings. They used this money to make more money. They invested in CD's, mutual funds and stocks. Now they just manage their portfolio and enjoy their retirement!

My brother, almost eleven years my senior, grew up in a much less lavish environment than I. Interestingly, he and my father are very similar. They are both CPAs. They are both very frugal, although my brother's frugality meter stays pegged "in the zone" constantly. He can pack away money with the best of them. He once found an apartment that only charged $40/month for rent, and that included utilities! He has always been great at finding deals. I can remember several times when he would literally pull the car over while driving because he was so good at spotting money on the shoulder of the road! I can remember him coming back to the car with a $5, $10 or occasionally a $20! He also invested in his own education and took advantage of his employer's education reimbursement program. After years of evening classes, he earned his master's degree in accounting. This allowed him to obtain a higher paying job and save more money. He and my father both learned how to be successful investors, and both did very well in the stock market. As a result, my father and brother both retired wealthy. My brother retired at the ripe old age of 48! Although they are both very intelligent and both had respectable incomes, it was their ability to save and invest wisely that allowed them to retire wealthy. I know many people who earn higher incomes than my father and brother did, but they will be working many years longer just because they do not have the commitment to invest their earnings instead of spending it!

My father-in-law, who did not have the luxury of a four year college education, is a tremendously successful person. He built a real estate and leasing company and ultimately co-owned several office buildings that he built for and leased to a national stock brokerage firm, telecommunication and insurance corporations, and several federal government agencies. Other investments he co-owns are some marinas and numerous residential vacant lots. How did he amass so much wealth? Frugality, among others, was a key factor.

My father-in-law has such an interesting life story. He was very careful with his money. No matter how much (or little) he earned, he put away a large percentage in savings in order to build for the future. He had a talent for repairing motorcycles and with enough savings parlayed that into owning a Harley Davidson dealership. After experiencing recurring problems from an old motorcycle injury, he had to give up riding. He just couldn't bear to be around all those motorcycles and not ride them, so he looked for another career. After ten years of ownership, he had to sell the Harley dealership. He interviewed several commercial real estate agents to handle the sale of the business, but did not agree with their methods of marketing. He immediately started taking real estate courses, obtained his license, and sold the business himself! He thought the process of selling his Harley dealership was relatively simple, so he decided to start selling real estate. First he started selling commercial businesses, then commercial buildings, then residential homes, commercial leasing, etc. Soon he was looking to open his own real estate brokerage firm. He found a great corner location that had more space (and a higher price tag) than he originally wanted. Many people would have splurged and taken the building and used all of the space for their business, with the idea of eventually filling in the space as their business grew. My father-in-law took a more frugal approach and sub-leased out the majority of the building, keeping only the minimal required space for his real estate business. The cash flow he generated from the leasing of the additional office space covered his mortgage payment for the entire building. He put any additional rental revenue toward the mortgage payments and paid off a twenty-five year mortgage in ten years!

A friend of mine is a financial advisor. He handles accounts for some NFL players along with some other wealthy clients. One of his clients was a mortgage loan officer who made upwards of $500,000 annually during the strong years of the real estate boom. One day he called his financial advisor asking for advice on filing bankruptcy. Most people would think that half a million dollars a year would be enough to retire on after a few years. What had happened? Why was this talented person now facing bankruptcy? In a nutshell, failure to be frugal. He lived the high life like it was never going to end. He bought the expensive sports car, he lived in a house well beyond his means, and he was not careful with his money. He made bad investments with his money and when the market slowed, it all came crashing down around him.

I have met several medium sized business owners that reached their position by working their way up from within the company. I was in San Diego one day auditing a successful appliance retail business that consistently delivered strong profits and was growing at a steady pace. The showrooms at each of the separate locations were all immaculate and boasted the latest product lines. I went into the owner's office at the headquarters and half expected to see beautiful back offices. Instead, the owner was set up in a small office. He badly needed more file cabinets and storage space. He was dressed neatly, but very modestly, wearing jeans and an ironed shirt. He invited me in and told me about how he worked his way up and eventually saved enough to purchase the business from the previous owners. They had gone through a downturn in the business and he thought he could take the business over and turn it around. What's the difference between him and other bright managers that could easily run their respective businesses? This guy had the conviction to save away the funds necessary to purchase the company. I've met several people like him over the years. They started out in lower management and SAVED enough to buy the business while learning the ropes.

Most financially successful people that practice frugality value the idea of TVM, the Time Value of Money. This enables your money to *work for you*. It's great to squirrel that money away, but what do you do with it? Put it in a safe deposit box? That won't even allow you to keep up with the rate of inflation. The idea behind TVM is investing a certain amount of your money in something that will earn you a certain rate of interest over a certain amount of time. The idea is you want to maximize the return on your money invested, preferably with as little risk as possible. The more money you invest and the longer you invest it, the more opportunity you give your money to *work for you*. The investment can be anything. It can be a certificate of deposit, a government bond, a share of stock, a mutual fund, a venture capital proposal, or your cousin that wants to start a doggie day care center and poochie spa. Various investments offer different rates of return along with corresponding levels of risk. While you can't always control the interest rate, you can usually control the other two variables, the amount of money and amount of time it is invested. Financially savvy individuals will keep as much money in their control for as long as possible. On a small scale, say you and your significant other decide to cut out on that daily café latte that costs you $3.00 each. At 30 purchases per person a month, that's $180/month savings between the two of you. If you just put the money under the mattress, after five years you have $10,800. If you place it in a low risk investment like a money market account earning 4% compounded monthly, at the end of five years you have $11,933.82. That's a significant amount of money for just dropping a frivolous habit. On a larger scale, the company I worked at within GE Capital had a policy of not paying their bills until at least 30 days out. Why? Because you can earn more money off of the money you keep in your control. The longer they kept their money, the more interest they made on it. They would tell their vendors in advance that their payments would be slow, but the vendors had no concern of GE going out of business anytime soon, so they often viewed it as an acceptable inconvenience. In the meantime, GE gets the opportunity to earn interest on tens of millions of dollars in accounts payable for an extra month at no cost to them. Of course they would want to pay their vendors slowly! On the flip side, while at GE Capital they had me run a Black Belt project focused on receiving our payments *sooner*. They understand TVM and dedicate a lot of resources to make sure they are in control of their money for as long as possible so they can squeeze every dollar they can out of their interest earned!

Buy low, sell high. Although this sounds simple enough, you wouldn't believe the individuals, small businesses and large corporations that get caught ignoring this rule. When Carlos Ghosn took over an ailing Nissan, one of the first things he did was restructure the relationship they had with their auto part suppliers. He felt they were paying too much for their parts, due to the tight relationships Nissan had with a relatively small number of suppliers. Mr. Ghosn opened up a more competitive environment and had multiple suppliers bid for jobs, driving down the parts costs and saving the company millions. In the US, this is the day and age of the big box retailer and virtual stores that give huge price cuts for a slew of products. And yet some people continue to purchase the same products in specialty stores paying top dollar. If it's just your everyday consumable items for the family or small business, do your best to plan periodic trips to your local big-box store. The savings are significant and add up over time. Utilize the internet to find the best deals. Use auction sites if you have to. Multiple, last-minute trips to a specialty or convenience store can drive up costs in a hurry. So many of the millionaires I know wear jeans, t-shirts and shorts as often as possible and look like anyone else walking along the street. They understand the value of keeping a dollar in their bank.

Buy when you aren't forced to buy and sell when you aren't forced to sell. Purchase that car, house or strip mall when the owner has to sell due to bankruptcy, divorce or job transfer. In the real estate market, don't be a sheep just moving along with the flock. If you buy when everyone else is buying and sell when everyone else is selling, you're probably buying at the top of the market and selling at the bottom of the market. When the market is down, I've watched savvy investors with money in the bank (which gives them spending power) scoop up real estate for pennies on the dollar. I've personally worked with banks to help them sell homes for 30% below market value. The educated investors in real estate wait for the market to drop then buy distressed sales instead of buying in the feeding frenzy of a market at its peak. Never let yourself get into the position of a forced sale – it's hard to watch those savvy buyers walk away with your property.

Frugality is difficult for most people. Americans are accustomed to spending close to or more than they bring home in after tax income. According to CNN Money.com, in 1985 Americans were saving more than 10% of their after tax take home pay. The savings rate slid from there and finally in 2005 it went into negative territory. Why? It's easy and fun. Being frugal is challenging and requires self discipline, while spending cash is easy and fun. The financially successful people have the will power to say no to the frivolous purchases. They are fine with driving a good looking, serviceable used car instead of opting for the new flashy sports car. They understand that reinvesting money into their business is essential to keep it operating. They understand that living beyond their means and having a negative savings rate is a recipe for disaster. Those that are able to master frugality reap the rewards of their efforts in the long run.

Think Outside of the Box

"It's important to have an open mind, but not so open that our brains fall out." – Sir Winston Churchill

Thinking outside of the box is a personal skill that is not easy for everyone to master. Coming up with ideas that are outside of the box requires some creative thinking. This thought process is often more indirect than straightforward and logical. This type of problem solving can be difficult for people with straightforward, logical mindsets. There are many exercises that can improve your ability to think outside of the box, but there is a definite gap between conducting these exercises in a controlled environment and using creative problem solving in the field.

Years ago I met a gentleman named Mike. He is the uncle of a good friend of mine, and an incredibly successful businessman who is tremendously wealthy. I spoke to him briefly at social functions over the years, but did not develop the relationship to have a serious conversation about his success until recent years. A few years ago, however, I was fortunate enough to have a private conversation with him and inquired about how he made his fortune. He got his start with a more traditional job in investment banking, then started looking for entrepreneurial opportunities. He told me about the airplane flight that changed his fortune from good to great. He was sitting on a plane and started a conversation with a passenger next to him. Eventually the conversation came to the inevitable "what do you do for a living" phase. The passenger stated he used to work for the government. His job involved assisting hospitals in recouping funds from state governments for various healthcare that was government funded. The passenger had since transferred jobs and now worked for the hospitals. He was paid as a sort of internal consultant that assisted the hospitals in recouping these expenses. He complained about being overworked and underpaid, as many people do from time to time. Mike thought for a moment and saw an opportunity. He asked how much money the passenger would be saving the hospital this year. The answer was in the millions. He asked if the hospitals would be open to paying a commission on the gross savings instead of hiring a consultant. The passenger thought it was a possibility. Mike quickly found other investors and, along with his newfound friend, developed a company which performed this necessary task. They took a percentage of the savings they were able to recoup from the government. Within a few years they were grossing in excess of $10 million. He was able to open his mind and envision a new paradigm. He wasn't afraid to take the leap of faith. A hundred things could have gone wrong with his business plan, but he took a shot at it and succeeded. His ability to think outside the box enabled him to react quickly to an opportunity. This was a niche that, at the time, very few people recognized. Often that is the doorway that gets people into the right position to become the industry leader.

When it comes to purchasing real estate, so many people think of the traditional forms of financing. They go to their bank or their traditional mortgage finance company. When my father-in-law purchased his first commercial building and sub-leased it to other business owners, he did this without traditional financing. He went to the owner of the building and asked for the owner to finance the sale of the property. This is simply called owner financing or a land contract. My father-in-law more than likely would not have been able to receive traditional financing at that stage in his life as he was just starting up a new business. He was able to convince the seller to give him a one year land contract, which gave him time to find tenants, obtain signed leases, and qualify for traditional bank financing. Creative thinking enabled him to get his first building and get his business jump started.

How many coworkers have you seen at work that do a good job, but never make it to the top? They just seem to blend in with all of their peers and never seem to jump out at you. When times are tough and the company needs to cut down on its payroll expenses, these are the people that find themselves on the cut list. How many businesses have you seen that blend in with the rest of the market and never differentiate themselves from the competition? These are the businesses that lack innovation and failed to think outside of the box. Without innovation, businesses are doomed to fail as their business model eventually becomes outdated.

Innovation is a key to running a successful business, no matter the size. When I was with GE Capital we had a system called GE Ideas. The company empowered any employee to submit their idea. Every recommendation was routed through a formal process by the Six Sigma quality group and given careful consideration. Frequently front line employees who were closest to the core business processes provided the best insight on fixing the problems.

Most of the successful businesses that I audited had a management team that focused on innovation. They stayed competitive in the marketplace by constantly reexamining and retuning their business model. Sometimes it was analyzing their sales and adjusting their product line to accommodate changes in consumer taste. Sometimes it was seeking out investors to inject much needed capital into their business in order to expand in the market. Sometimes it was staying ahead of the competition by being a forerunner in online sales. Whatever it was, the result was consistent. The winners were innovators.

Once I asked Ed Moldt, the billionaire, what his most profitable business was. He told me a story about a water treatment operation he built. He was sitting in his office with a colleague when the phone rang. The caller wanted to know if he knew anyone who could help with building a water treatment facility for a shopping center. They assured the caller that they could handle his request for building the plant and set up a time in the future to review the project with the customer. After they hung up the phone, they rushed around madly to try and learn how water treatment facilities are operated and constructed! They were able to pull everything together in time for the presentation and were awarded the contract to build the facility. They created an opportunity where none existed. They took a chance and could have fallen flat on their faces, but they worked hard to get up to speed on the project and were able to create a business. Not only did they build the facility, but they also operated it on an ongoing basis. Once it was up and running, it only took one employee to operate daily. He was pleasantly surprised at how lucrative this operation was. All it took was an open mind and some creative thinking and voila, they were in the water treatment business!

I recall another instance when Mr. Moldt spoke about looking for opportunities. He talked about how opportunities sometimes land right at your feet and you just have to be able to think creatively to recognize them. He went on to discuss how he was reading the newspaper in the morning and saw an article about an airline that was starting up. He noticed the name of the airline was the same name he had registered for one of his companies. He got on the phone with his attorney and eventually settled the dispute with the airline. Their oversight ultimately cost the airline one million dollars!

I consider innovation synonymous with thinking outside of the box. Successful companies consistently come up with ways of reinventing their business as the market changes. I know several successful business owners that like to take time during the slow season of the year and evaluate their business. They will identify what they have done correctly along with their failures, and they use this while formulating their business plan for the next year. They often use the following format while brainstorming ways to improve their business.

ELIMINATE   IMPROVE   MAINTAIN

This serves as a good starting point for evaluating processes that need to be eliminated, improved or retained. Some businesses like to reevaluate more frequently. For example, 3M used to challenge their employees to develop ideas for new products weekly. You never know when the next sticky note will be invented!

I watched the CEO of Google, Eric Schmidt, on CNN and absolutely loved his ideas on innovation. Google provides their employees with time to work on new ideas. They can take up to 20% of their work time to develop new ways of doing business. Mr. Schmidt went on to say they anticipate 90% of the ideas to fail, but it's worth it to be innovative and move forward with that 10% that succeed. He stressed that it's ok to fail. The important thing is the fact that if you keep trying to be innovative you will succeed.

Jack Welch spoke to us at GE one day about innovation. He talked about the importance of keeping up with the market and constantly reinventing our business. He brought up an example of a company that thought outside the box and adapted to the market quickly after the world trade center incident on 9/11/01. Airline passengers at the time were very wary of travelling on larger planes with the major airlines. Some owners of a smaller airline commuter service started offering short trips out of New York City to nearby regional airports. Jack didn't want us to feel like our company was so big that we could not adapt to change quickly. He wanted us to keep the mindset of a smaller company that could readily innovate new ideas to change and improve the business.

Investing Income

"Friendship is like money, easier made than kept." – Samuel Butler

I know an MD that has a very strong income. He's been working as a doctor for 20+ years. He is respected by his peers in the medical profession and if you asked his peers I'm sure they would say his career has been successful. He has most of the luxuries you would expect a doctor to have. He has the large house, the nice cars, and all the usual toys. He also has several children. He has a highly educated daughter who left the house, but is on welfare. He has another child in his twenties that will not leave the house, and has no real plans for generating any wealth in the near future. It's ironic that this doctor has worked and studied so hard to get to a position where he can earn such a strong income, and yet he really doesn't have that much wealth. He has debt from all his luxury items, and he has a few children who rely on him to provide for them, which is really another form of debt.

Unless he changes his ways, this brilliant man will spend the rest of his days working for his toys and those few difficult children. His mindset is to work hard, make a large paycheck, and spend his money on things that bring him instant gratification. When he raised these children, they adapted a similar mindset. However, due to a bad job market, laziness, or some other reason these children never generated any significant income. They did what they had been raised to do. They spent and did not save. They went back to the ATM, also known as dad, when they needed money or a place to live.

I've known several successful people who earned a strong salary but either did not understand how to invest their money or chose not to invest their money. They earned lots of money and spent lots of money. But when any life changing event came along they became financially distressed. Why? They never took the first step, which is to commit to investing. They never took the time to actually save up some equity for investing. The next step is selecting the type of investment and actually pulling the trigger. There are limitless possibilities. The investment can be stocks, bonds, a business, venture capital, real estate, etc. The last step is managing the investment.

Choosing the type of investment that's right for you can be difficult. I've seen successful executives assume that because they are successful in their business they will be successful in managing a real estate investment. Many of them have been wrong and have lost their shirts because they either did not understand or ignored the amount of time required for the venture. I'll go into much more detail concerning real estate later in the book. There are so many fascinating ways to invest in real estate that I dedicated an entire section to it. Several investments can be time consuming. Many opportunities such as building or buying a business and purchasing commercial or residential rental property can typically require more time than investing in stocks, bonds or REITs (Real Estate Investment Trust). The successful investors I've known had investment strategies that matched their lifestyles. For example, most successful real estate investors and business owners I know work locally in the area near their investments and had the required flexibility to attend to them when necessary. An executive who is required to relocate frequently or travel constantly will find it more challenging to keep on top of an operation like this from afar. It's not impossible, but the people I know that do this rely heavily on their local management team. Someone on the go constantly and working 60 hours a week may do well to stick with the stock market. Think long and hard about your present work situation and the amount of flexibility you have before you invest in anything.

Let's face it. It's hard to be great at everything. It's asking a lot to think someone can spend most of her waking hours striving to be one of the best brain surgeons in the city and also expect that person to be great at investing money. It's a stretch to think that a single mother raising two children and working double shifts can have the time to go out during the day and search for real estate investments. As our society changes, more households are turning into dual income households where both spouses work. Employees are spending more time at work. Some of the wealthy people I've worked with had the time to research their investments on their own, but many did not have that luxury. When it comes to making money, the vast majority of wealthy people I know stick to what they do best. They are specialists who have honed their skills over the years. They have advanced within their field and over time made more and more money as they improved their service. They make their money by working as a doctor, attorney, business owner, executive at a large corporation, etc. When they want to invest money in something outside of their realm of expertise, they do what large corporations have been doing for years; they outsource it. When an automobile mechanic needs a root canal, he doesn't go to the world's smartest neurosurgeon. He goes to a dentist that has experience with root canals. When a neurosurgeon wants to invest her money in commercial real estate, she doesn't go to an automobile mechanic. She goes to a real estate broker that handles commercial real estate. When wealthy people invest their money, they look for a specialist.

As a real estate broker, I attracted a lot of wealthy people to my office that were looking to invest in real estate. I stood out from my peers because of my MBA and prior experience as a real estate investor. My customers wanted advice from someone who specialized in the industry. They would typically provide me with guidelines of what they were looking for such as: price range, zoning, property use, risk tolerance, geographic location, size of the property and number of units, tax benefits, cash flow projections, price appreciation projections, etc. I would do a lot of research, and then contact them to review my findings. From there we would usually narrow it down a bit more and set a date to go view the remaining properties. I would meet my customer when it was convenient for his schedule. This allowed him to keep earning an income in his specialty, without the search for a real estate investment slowing him down. As a real estate broker I've worked with many corporate executives, doctors, attorneys, CPAs, business owners, financial advisors, finance managers, leasing managers, asset managers, and generally a lot of people that are much more intelligent than I am. Why do they pick up the phone and call me? Because they are about to invest a lot of money in real estate and they want someone with years of real estate investment experience assisting them. I've even had owners of other real estate investment firms utilize my services because they were looking for someone with my specific knowledge base and experience. Likewise, when I want to invest in the stock market, set up a Roth IRA, or revisit my retirement investment strategy, I don't do it myself. I call someone who specializes in wealth management. Most wealthy people earn their money by focusing on one specific industry or function. When they want to invest, they select a field in which to invest their money and then choose an expert within their targeted field to assist them with the investment.

Do you want to be hands on and do the investing yourself? I've certainly known several people that were able to go that route and come out winners, but they were the ones who were cautious in their investment strategies and had the time to devote to managing their portfolios. My brother (remember the one that retired at the age of 48?) managed his own investment portfolio. He committed the time to do it and committed to a conservative strategy. He started out by investing in utility and big oil stocks.

Later he diversified into blue chip stocks. When the stock market went into a frenzy between 1997 – 2000, he diverted his investments away from stocks. Instead of sending more money into the stock market, he used it to pay off debt. He wasn't sucked into the stock market bubble where stocks like Krispy Kreme Doughnuts were soaring upward with a P/E (price-earnings ratio) of 60. To put this into perspective, the P/E ratio for the DOW Index was 15.5 at the time this book was written. He did lose money on some stocks. When he did take a loss, he would sell the stocks and take advantage of the tax write off as a long term loss. He would wait 30+ days, as required by the IRS, and then buy the same stocks again.

We've reviewed committing to make an investment, selecting an investment, and now I am going to discuss managing the investment. For the purpose of this section, when I refer to managing I am referring to the practice of reviewing your investment portfolio and making those critical decisions to keep it in line with your objectives. Do you need to liquidate it? Is it too risky for your taste? Is the risk level associated with it in alignment with your goals? If it's a short term investment, it should be low risk. A high risk portfolio is better suited for a long term investment. Is the portfolio diversified? Is the portfolio too heavily weighted in one or more sectors and in need of realignment? You can mitigate risk within your portfolio through diversification. These sound like pretty basic strategies, but most of the people I know that lost a significant amount of invested money did so by ignoring these basic guidelines. The people I know that lost the most were the ones that failed to diversify.

Risk can actually be measured with an equation. Diversifying the portfolio of investments is one of the best ways to reduce the risk of the portfolio. For example, too much of any one stock can make the portfolio more susceptible to volatility. Volatility allows the value to fluctuate. Eventually, practically everyone needs to liquidate part of their portfolio. You don't want to be one month away from retirement and find out that 20% of your retirement portfolio has been wiped out because is was susceptible to volatility! I have seen too many wealthy, intelligent individuals lose a fortune by not diversifying!

I once had a very intelligent and highly educated sales agent that worked for me named Rob. Rob had his MBA and not only sold real estate, but he also ran the Florida branch of a land development company based out of Denver. When the land development market crashed in 2008, one of the senior partners of the Denver firm took a devastating loss to his net worth. Why? He had everything invested in real estate. He never took the time to diversify in other markets. Don't let it happen to you! On the flip side of the coin, I've seen business owners use diversification to their advantage. I've seen several successful real estate brokers diversify their revenue sources by competing in commercial sales, residential sales, commercial leasing, residential leasing, or a combination of these. The upside of this strategy is if the residential market takes a dive, they would already be established in the commercial market. If property sales took a dive then they could focus on property management, and so on.

Committing to the *idea* of investing your wealth and *actually* investing it are key to gaining momentum and building upon your financial success. Without investing, it's like being on a treadmill that never stops. You can make all the money you want, but if you don't invest you can't take a break and you have to keep running on that treadmill! Diversification and active management of your investments are critical to building your wealth and giving it the best opportunity to work for you!

A Note on Lending Money

"I hope that after I die, people will say of me: That guy sure owed me a lot of money." – Jack Handey

A joke I often heard was GE is the world's largest non-bank bank. They have loads of money to lend through their various financial institutions, and yet they are not a bank. If you are asked to make a personal loan to a family member, friend or business partner, make sure you collateralize the loan and obtain the services of <u>your</u> attorney when drawing up the payment schedule, balloon payments, valuation method of the collateral, and all other applicable terms. If you are going to hand out your hard earned money you better receive a good rate of return on it and you better have some collateral (cash, car, boat, house, stocks, etc.) that you can collect in case the debt cannot be repaid. How much is a good rate of return? It really depends on the risk of the loan, but it should be more than what you could earn by putting the money in a low risk money market account or CD. Remember, you may be spending your valuable time trying to collect on the loan down the road.

Verbal contracts are worth about as much as the paper they're written on, which is nothing. Put everything in writing and have all parties involved sign all documentation. If there are any changes, write up new documentation or an addendum and have everyone sign. No exceptions! GE demands sufficient collateral and signatures on paperwork, and so should you. Assume the worst case scenario that you will be in court fighting for repayment of your loan or fighting for possession of the collateral. Even the fortune 500 companies have the wool pulled over their eyes from time to time and come up empty-handed when trying to collect on a loan.

VOC & CTQ

I will discuss Six Sigma later in the book, but I'll take some time now to introduce these terms, voice of the customer (VOC) and critical to quality (CTQ).

I had just met my father-in-law when he was building his first building for the U.S. Government. These contracts were difficult to obtain. The General Services Administration (GSA) required quite a bit of detail to go into the bidding process. There were several other contractors and developers bidding for this contract due to the fact that GSA leases were very secure and non-cancellable. I asked him how he was able to get the GSA to award him such a great contract. He started by treating the government like a valuable customer, and he realized that it is important to understand what the customer wants. At GE we called it VOC, or voice of the customer. At GE, we were focused on cutting through the layers of opinions everyone seemed to have about what the customer wanted and needed. We would go directly to the source and get the opinions from the end users. This is exactly what my father-in-law did. He did a tremendous amount of research into what the GSA wanted and visited several existing government buildings to research the various types of construction and design. My father-in-law asked "What are the most important factors for you regarding your new building?" They were looking for a building that had a safe and secure location and design. Now he understood the critical element of what the customer wanted. At GE we called this the customer's CTQ. It's the requirement that is critical to quality. How did he satisfy the customer's CTQ? He searched for a site that provided safety and security. He found a vacant parcel located at the end of two streets with no vehicle access on two sides of the property. He submitted the site to the GSA and they approved it. He did not have enough construction and development experience to handle the project on his own, so he decided to contact the largest and most reputable building firm in the area. He spoke with the owner and told him of his plans to obtain a bid from the GSA. The owner said, "You'll never win that bid. I've tried before and never won the bid." He had joined the group of naysayers that give up after the first rejection. My father-in-law worked out a scenario where he and the builder would work as partners if they won the bid. After working together for four years and submitting several revised bids they were awarded the GSA contract and have been partners ever since.

After the success story with the first building, they started submitting bids to the GSA for other government buildings. He and his partners were later awarded three more GSA firm leases and built two more office buildings. It all started with something very simple, listening to your customer and understanding what is critical for your customer.

The Sears Roebuck and Co. leadership team understood and preached the importance of knowing who your customer is. Similarly, GE ingrained customer service into its management team. When I first joined GE it was the "Year of the Customer." I thought, "Wow this is a terrific idea on how to remind the entire company the importance of customer service." I think the next year was also the "Year of the Customer." I also believe my third year there was another "Year of the Customer." The campaign was repetitive and effective. Everything was focused on the VOC and CTQ. I can't overemphasize how the company drove customer centered behavior. They never wanted any employee to forget how important our customers were.

How do you obtain your VOC and CTQ? In most cases, you simply ask your customer. Surveys, feedback forms and focus groups are all great ways to get your hands on that ever so critical VOC! In some instances, an employee that is very close to the customer can provide helpful insight to the customer needs. Usually this is a sales rep or account rep that is closely tied to the customer and understands the problems they deal with on a daily basis. Be careful about using an internal employee's opinion as your exclusive source of VOC. The best information is straight from the customer's mouth.

Many companies do not use the exact terms VOC and CTQ. If you polled employees from 100 different companies you may only find a small percentage that knows what these acronyms mean. While these acronyms may be specific to Six Sigma or other quality programs, the concept is universal. *You need to pay attention to your customer needs or your customers will disappear.*

Economies of Scale

The Merriam-Webster dictionary defines economies of scale as a reduction in the cost of producing something brought about especially by increased size of production facilities. Economies of scale occur if the average cost per unit decreases by expanding production. In other words, they occur if doubling your output is accompanied by less than doubling your input. Take for example a small bakery that produces cupcakes. The owner has a handful of employees and current expenses are $200,000 annually. She can add another employee without having to alter or expand the current manufacturing facility. Wages, insurance and benefits for one additional production line worker will cost her $40,000. She estimates the worker can boost production by 20,000 cupcakes annually.

Current Expenses	Units Produced	Cost/Unit
$200,000	50,000	$4.00

Adding 1st Employee

Expenses	Units Produced	Cost/Unit	Decrease in Unit Cost
$240,000	70,000	$3.43	14%

You can see adding one employee greatly increases production with a minimal increase in overhead cost. This leads to a decrease in the cost per unit of production and economies of scale are achieved. Note the significant decrease in unit cost of 14%. As long as she can sell and distribute all of the additional cupcakes produced, the owner would do well to keep expanding production. Here are the numbers with the next additional employee.

Adding 2nd Employee

Expenses	Units Produced	Cost/Unit	Decrease in Unit Cost
$280,000	87,000	$3.22	6%

As she adds more employees, she finds the production facility getting cramped, so she estimates a diminishing return in production with each worker added. With this in mind, she estimates the 2nd additional employee will only be able to increase production by 17,000 units instead of 20,000. Each successive employee added will have a slightly lower impact than the previous one. The bakery owner, wanting to take advantage of economies of scale, will keep adding additional employees to decrease her cost per unit. The decrease in cost gives her a competitive advantage over similar bakeries that are smaller in scale. However, if she keeps adding employees she will eventually get to a point of diminishing returns, where adding one additional employee starts to increase the cost/unit of production. There is only so much room in her bakery for employees to operate. Too many employees in a cramped space will slow down production quickly. With additional employees also comes the need for more management. With a little planning she can find the right balance of employees and managers to optimize productivity in her factory, and then look at the cost benefit of expanding to a larger facility.

Another example of economies of scale is purchasing in bulk. A company can typically decrease their cost of purchasing supplies when they agree to purchase bulk quantities. This allows them to produce more without increasing the amount spent on supplies, or input. Another example of economies of scale is specialization of labor. Larger companies tend to allow workers to specialize more in a task. As a worker becomes more specialized, she becomes more of an expert and becomes more productive. Increased scale of production also leads to technical advantages. For example, a large automobile manufacturer may have the ability to automate several of their processes with machines, which can lead to improved processes and productivity. Finally, smaller companies may not be able to utilize all of their skills and abilities of their management staff, while large companies have greater opportunity to utilize more of their skills and services. You can see why there is certainly an advantage of being big. Wal-Mart, Chevron, Home Depot, and Honda are all stellar examples of economies of scale at work.

I've mentioned the term productivity a few times thus far. I'm sure everyone has a general understanding that productivity is a good attribute and generally has a positive connotation. Most people would think it means making the best use of one's time. I'm sure you're thinking, "Ok, the employees can be more productive with their time if they specialize in a process." That is correct, but I think it's worth spending a little time expanding on the term productivity, especially as it relates to economies of scale. Productivity describes the number of units produced over a certain amount of time. For an auto manufacturer it can be expressed as the number of cars produced per day. For a bank it can be expressed as the number of loans originated per month. It's a way to measure a company's output over time. When looking at ways to grow a business, making your current employees more productive is much more attractive than adding employees or increasing the size of your current production facility. That's why productivity measures are scrutinized, tweaked and massaged constantly. Increased productivity is what companies need in order to thrive. It's one of the primary reasons management exists. It's one of the differentiators between companies that succeed and those that fail.

I have another acquaintance who owns several hotels in a relatively concentrated geographic area. He utilizes economies of scale by selecting one manager to watch over multiple hotels, rather than paying for multiple managers. For simplicity purposes, imagine three hotel managers managing three separate hotels, each earning $75,000. Total salaries for all three are $225,000. Compare this to one manager overseeing three hotels with a salary of $125,000. I saw this routinely happen at GE Capital. An underperforming manager would be released and the group he managed would be reorganized under another manager's group. Believe it or not, this was actually looked upon favorably by the new manager absorbing the employees. She now had much more responsibility and an opportunity to prove herself worthy of the challenge, often without any increase in pay at all.

My friend, Jimmy, who started his fortune with convenience stores and gas stations, utilized economies of scale to his advantage. With the large number of stores he had accumulated, he could utilize his size and strength in the local market to his advantage. His relatively large amount of purchasing power gave him more negotiating leverage with suppliers. Suppliers, egar to place products in 10 stores instead of just one, would offer price discounts and incentives for the opportunity to get more volume on his shelves. Once he acquired a sizeable portfolio of stores, he was able to utilize volumes of data from each of the locations and build a statistical model for predicting performance. The model could also be used for determining the price of a target store for sale. Economy of scale also allowed him to better utilize his managers. He could pick the most productive individual store managers and promote them to manage multiple stores instead of just one. This enabled him to cut down on his labor costs just like the hotel owner previously mentioned.

I saw several businesses leverage economies of scale to their advantage in the appliance retail industry. They would expand and grow, gaining clout and bargaining power with the appliance manufacturers. I watched many successful appliance dealers expand locally and regionally. With each expansion they were able to better utilize their managers, make better use of technology on a large scale, and squeeze their suppliers for lower prices. Interestingly, in the appliance industry I also saw several small to mid sized companies forced out of business due to a national chain moving into their local market. Lowes and Home Depot frequently were the cause for relatively smaller appliance retailers closing their doors. The economy of scale wielded by the national big box stores can easily crush smaller competitors once they enter a market.

Dominate the Market

Domination of the market dovetails with economies of scale because it's much easier to dominate the market if you have a size advantage. Home Depot and Lowes tend to dominate their local markets due to economies of scale. The small to mid level hardware stores in their markets struggle to compete with them. The buying and negotiating power of a national powerhouse like Home Depot can easily crush local competition in a local market through use of economies of scale. Domination of the market doesn't always require economies of scale, however. In this section I will not dwell on dominating the national market, but instead dominating the relatively smaller markets.

In selling real estate, I quickly learned that it was much easier and often more profitable to focus on a small niche market. I know owners of real estate brokerage firms and agents that, for a variety of reasons, cast a wide net and compete across multiple markets, often covering several counties. They have to cover a large territory, which means they have to spend a significant amount of time in the car going back and forth between counties or cities as they serviced all their customer needs. The firms that employ this strategy rarely dominate their local market because they are spread too thin. An agent in this setting may spend up to several hours each day commuting between customers. Compare this to an agent or firm that focuses on a handful of neighborhoods within a two mile radius of their office. The time saved in commuting alone gives these agents a competitive advantage.

Dominating a smaller niche market also allows you to more readily become an expert in that market. Focusing on a neighborhood market requires less research time to become an expert than focusing on the entire city, county or state. Being the insider in your local market can be an advantage. The competitors that are viewed as outsiders often find it more difficult to break into a market dominated by a local businessperson. It is also easier to keep a pulse on a smaller market. Relatively speaking, learning which competitors are having health problems, financial problems, employee problems, landlord disputes, etc. and using that information to your advantage is much easier if you're focusing on a 4 mile radius rather than a 40 mile radius.

I know several managers of a company that owns a local hospital and several rehabilitation clinics. They control a very large market share of the in patient rehabilitation and compete strongly in out patient rehabilitation. They do a great job of dominating this market in northeast FL. Previous attempts of expanding to the west portion of the state and expanding north into GA have proven difficult. Managing remote employees and dealing with the legal requirements of another state are challenges that keep them focused on dominating the northeast FL market rather than expanding to different regions.

Even if you dominate your local market, you need to keep your business poised for stiff competition. A large majority of the failing businesses I audited with GE had a competitor move in to the area and take away too much of the market share. In most cases these competitors were big box companies leveraging their economies of scale. A secondary reason for a business failing was a downturn in the local economy due to local plant or business closings. These plant shutdowns would lead to the local labor force relocating and therefore a reduction in the customer base. The businesses that failed had no contingency plan and were caught with their guard down. One minute they were dominating the market and the next they were closing their doors. The ones that were able to withstand these market changes were the ones that had diversified business models, such as internet sales, to insulate themselves from competition and downturns in the local economy.

In the section Invest in Yourself, I mentioned a banker who owned a large portfolio of townhomes. One of the reasons he has been so successful is his ability to keep a pulse on the relatively small market he targets. He spent years mailing letters to townhome owners, offering to purchase if they were in a difficult position and needed to sell. Over the years, word of mouth, along with his continuous direct mail marketing plan, helped him become recognized as a resource for distressed sales. At the time I wrote this section, he had recently picked up a distressed 2 bedroom 2 bath townhome with minimal repairs needed for just over $25,000. By dominating this local area, he has put himself in a position where he is one of the first points of contact when someone needs to sell a distressed townhome.

My previously mentioned friend, Jimmy, also utilizes this technique in his gas station / convenience store business. He sometimes leased his gas stations from the oil companies and sometimes purchased the real estate. Occasionally he would purchase as much property as possible in a small market. One example of him using this tactic is a small but strategic intersection in a very small town. There were gas station/convenience stores on three of the four corners and a commercial business on the fourth. He eventually purchased the land on all four corners of the intersection. Even though this was only a small "microcosm" of the marketplace, it's nice not to have to worry about competition across the street! He kept his ear to the ground and jumped on opportunities to purchase commercial real estate in the vicinity of this intersection. He purchased older buildings at lower prices that were in need of repair and would rehab them. With the new facelift, he could demand a higher rent and generate positive cash flow then move on to the next acquisition. As he grew his commercial property portfolio, he was able to utilize economies of scale. The more properties he had listed for sale or for rent, the more contacts and prospective buyers/renters he had. As he purchased more and more commercial buildings, he grew his network of tenants and buyers. At the time this book was written, the most recent commercial strip center he built had tenants in place for each of the spaces prior to construction of the building! That's a great way to mitigate risk for a commercial landlord and a huge weight off of any landlord's chest.

It's easy to see how dominating the market and economies of scale are intertwined, but my intent in this section was to show how even a one man operation can dominate the marketplace without having a national chain providing economies of scale!

Persistence

"Never give in! Never give in! Never, never, never, never - in nothing great or small, large or petty. Never give in except to convictions of honor and good sense." - Sir Winston Churchill

I spent some time working as a consultant for Dave Pawlak, co-owner of a business and also a good friend of mine. Before starting his business, Dave went through the traditional four year business school, worked in the mortgage banking industry for a while, and then worked for a start up company in the semiconductor industry. Unfortunately the business ended up failing. Instead of feeling sorry for himself, Dave saw an opportunity where others saw failure. Owing millions to creditors, the business owners were considering filing for bankruptcy. Dave came up with a solution to handle liquidating all the assets and the renegotiating the lease the company had on their building. The lease alone represented $1.2 million in debt. He was able to renegotiate the lease down to $120,000. This savings, along with the money he was able to recoup by selling off the equipment, enabled the owners to stay out of bankruptcy court and keep a black mark off of their credit history. Dave was also rewarded financially for his efforts. He turned a dire situation into a win-win situation! He made additional income, the owners did not have to file bankruptcy, and Dave immersed himself in a new market for semiconductor fabrication equipment. While he was finding buyers on the secondary market for semiconductor equipment, he met a contact and they later started their own business, Class One Equipment. Their business model is to purchase used or non-functional semiconductor fabrication equipment then refurbish and sell it. He was able to live out of the West Coast, and later the Midwest, while setting up a refurbishing plant in Georgia. He travels around the U.S. and overseas looking for companies that have excess semiconductor fabrication equipment. Other partners oversee the refurbishing process and the sale of the final product. Due to his persistence, Dave was able to turn failure into an opportunity. He is now part owner of a very successful company after rising from the ashes of a failed company!

Previously I mentioned Ed Moldt, the billionaire professor of mine. He has a fascinating history. Ed started his career in the traditional way in corporate America and made his way to the top of the corporate ladder at Philip Morris. He was relatively young, well-off and able to retire. He had a Rolls Royce, a nice home and nothing but time on his hands as he started his entrepreneurial adventure. Unfortunately his first business decision involved taking a huge financial risk that went belly up. He partnered with some investors that purchased the Queen Elisabeth and attempted to convert the ship into a tourist attraction in Port Everglades, FL. The plan sounded solid. Purchase a ship that has name recognition around the world, bring it to Florida and turn it into a tourist attraction. Souvenirs could be made of the existing equipment all over the ship. They could make key chains out of mooring lines. Everyday items could be turned into a collectible – you get the picture. At the time, Disneyworld was a newly created success in the area. Why not follow their model? Unfortunately this fantastic idea did not pan out. Expenses rose, timelines were delayed, and the ship was eventually shut down as a fire hazard.[1] Shortly thereafter the parent company owning the ship filed for bankruptcy.[2]

Ed was devastated and left broke. In the matter of a few years he watched his fortune, retirement, everything evaporate. Remember the previous section on the risk of not diversifying your investment portfolio? It can happen to even the savviest entrepreneur. What would this loss do to the average person? It would crush them. Instead of wallowing in self-pity, Ed hit the streets looking for work. He landed a job at Sears Roebuck selling shirts. I recall Ed telling us his story about the Sears job. My jaw hit the floor. He wanted to make sure every customer left the store with a shirt. From rock bottom there was only one way to go, and that was straight up. He started hitting the streets and looking for a real estate opportunity. He assisted in putting together a real estate deal for a church. This led to another job some ministers offered him which entailed running a home for the mentally handicapped. This position could be seen as a consuming challenge to some, but Ed turned it into an opportunity. From this one business, he eventually created several offshoot companies. As an example, he created his own leasing company to service the transportation needs of the handicapped home. Instead of building and selling businesses, Ed tends to build and keep them, then keep building. That first home for the mentally handicapped later turned into a business involving well over 100 homes.[3]

Instead of yielding to failure, Ed showed persistence and came out a winner. He just kept his nose to the grindstone and looked for opportunities. Once he got the first business going, he looked for more opportunities and just kept looking for the next business to start! Success is a process. Unfortunately, success is often a *slow* process! Millionaires are typically not made overnight. It takes intestinal fortitude to pick yourself up, dust yourself off, and keep trying. Persistence is easier said than done. Getting rejected or suffering a business failure is something that many people cannot tolerate. Those who are persistent can overcome and reap the benefits!

Strategic Relationships

"It's not *what* you know, but *who* you know that's important."

You hear about it all the time. Fortune 500 companies creating alliances to benefit strategically from each other's strengths. Microsoft works out a deal with Verizon to expand their footprint of mobile search queries.[4] Best Buy partners with Carphone Warehouse Plc to compete better in cell phone sales.[5] You also see cities vie for sporting events such as the Super Bowl, the Olympics, or a basketball tournament in order to bring in more revenue, and promote their brand name and awareness.

A lot of people think their small or medium sized business doesn't have the clout to really develop strategic relationships.

There are plenty of opportunities out there, and successful people do a great job of exploiting them. On a smaller scale, an acquaintance of mine that owns an NFL sports management firm partnered with an R&B producer to help bring in more athletes. The NFL athletes generally like R&B, and most look favorably upon an opportunity to hang out with some celebrities in the music industry! Likewise, the R&B producer's clients tend to enjoy hanging out with athletes. It's a mutually beneficial situation.

As I mentioned previously, my friend Brett, who co-owns the hotel and resort, went out and found the right people to build a strategic relationship with. He had the knowledge, ability and time to run the operation. They had the money. He convinced them that he could manage the property at a relatively low salary, but he wanted a share in ownership of the company. It was a win-win situation.

I've witnessed several Realtors pick up and move to a more affluent neighborhood. The new territory they now market to has higher priced real estate. Since the agents work on commission, their commission check for each sale is now larger than it was previously. They are not doing anything drastically different. They are just marketing to a higher income client and creating a new strategic relationship that will result in relatively higher earnings than the previous one.

The same theory holds true for people working in Fortune 500 companies. At GE Capital, I once worked for a very sharp senior manager, Wanda Sturm. One of her talents was the ability to look beyond a problem and understand the strategic political picture. She would consistently move Six Sigma projects forward by being able to massage and manipulate (in a positive way) the key stakeholders on the projects. She created win-win scenarios for managers that would work with her and help her bring projects to successful completion. Later, she was able to parlay this successful track record into another successful career at Hewlett-Packard.

I have a very financially successful friend, Jim, who is the manager of a UBS office. He has a number of financial advisors that work for him at his office, which primarily deals with wealth management. Several years ago, we were diving in the keys for a few days of vacation. I started talking about expanding my real estate firm and welcomed any advice he could offer. In a nutshell, the typical real estate brokers keep a portion of the revenue generated by each agent. There are different variations on compensation, but usually the more the agents sell, the more the brokers make. Increasing the number of agents gives brokers more opportunity to make more money. He gave me some advice that at first seemed silly, but really made sense. Over the years it has stuck with me just because of the simplicity of the statement. He said, "You need to find the right person." I thought, "Ok, that's stating the obvious." He said, "You don't want 1+1 to equal 2. You want 1+1 to equal 3." I was beginning to think it was a mistake to bring up this topic. He continued, "You don't want to just bring in a volume of agents that will slow you down with training, managing and mentoring added to your schedule and not get the productivity from them in return. You want to bring in the agents that will exponentially increase your revenue stream." He was right, of course. It's easy to get into the rut of hiring more agents, training more agents, paying the overhead for more agents, doing more work that is associated with having a larger firm, mentoring more agents, and eventually firing more agents and having more agents quit because they are not getting enough attention from the broker. Jim was prodding me to look at the big picture. He wanted me to look at the strategic move. Anyone can just work more and make more money. He was reminding me that the successful business owners leverage relationships and find the right relationships that will exponentially build wealth for the business.

The financially successful business owners and managers choose their business partners wisely. They don't look for quantity alone. They look for quality over quantity. They don't look for relationships that are going to slow down the business by creating more bureaucracy. They look for partners that can unite strengths and develop a combination that is greater than the sum of the parts. They look for 1+1 to equal 3!

Recruiting and Developing Talented Managers

So many wealthy businesspeople rely on strong managers or key employees to assist in running the business. In large operations it is essential to have a staff with some talent on it to keep the operation running smoothly. Even in a small firm the person running the show, be that the CEO, president, managing partner, general manager, or someone with another title, needs to have a strong support cast to assist in running the daily operations so the leader can focus on long term objectives and strategic planning. I witnessed general managers of hardware and appliance stores run themselves ragged trying to do all the day to day operations. This works fine in the short term, but if they spend all their time managing the day to day operations and not focusing on the strategic marketing and business plan, the operation is doomed. I saw more than one business fail because of the general manager's inability to recruit and develop a strong management staff.

Recruiting talent is closely related to developing strategic relationships. For instance, my friend Jim, the manager at UBS, is great at building strategic relationships. Some of those relationships are clients, and some are employees. He has a great ability to recruit talented financial advisors. This is what makes him extremely valuable to the company and correspondingly allows him to demand a higher salary. Jim is able to bring in talented financial advisors, who in turn make millions for the company. Bringing in the most talented financial advisors gives his business group a strong competitive advantage.

You can see the same relationship between recruiting and having a competitive advantage in sports. Take football as an example. In the 1994 season, the NFL needed to institute a salary cap to try and keep a select few teams from bringing in too much talent and dominating the league for a prolonged time. The same relationship exists in college football. Compare the top perennial 25 recruiting teams in the nation with the perennial top 25 poll rankings and you will see a strong correlation. Recruiting talent gives you a tremendous advantage.

Consider Ed Moldt, the billionaire that owned close to 200 businesses. How did he juggle the operations management of all of these companies? He delegates to his managers. He segmented the companies out and hired high quality managers to run the various groups. He didn't seem to micromanage his managers. He would rather start a business, then let someone else run the day to day operations. This way he could focus on starting the next business. He stated that he would ask for just a few pieces of information from each business unit leader. However, he would ask for the information daily. He tended to leave them alone as long as there were no negative trends developing and profitability was steady or improving. He used a snapshot of metrics, or measurements, to get a picture of how each business was performing. I will discuss metrics in greater detail later in the book. Ed stated he did not flinch when one of his business unit leaders would come in and ask for a raise. He just wanted them to justify how they were going to increase profitability in the near future to justify the salary increase. One day in class, he stated he paid one of his managers upwards of $200,000 annually. I asked him for a job that day after our session. He politely informed me that he wasn't in need of a manager at the present time. What can I say? I had to jump at a fantastic opportunity like that!

So how did Ed interview and select his managers? Obviously it wasn't by picking out his ambitious students! He would bring each recruit in and spend lots of time with them, sometimes several days to get to know them. He told us a story once about a candidate that he took out golfing. He made sure to set him up with a separate group and made a small wager with the candidate on the game. In this group was a trusted employee that would report back to Ed at the end of the day. Among other items, he would report back on how honest the candidate was with his golf game. This particular candidate felt the need to cheat a little during the game. Needless to say, he did not get the position. Ed felt that if he couldn't trust him with a few dollars on the line, how could he trust him with running a business with potentially millions on the line? On another occasion, he decided not to hire a candidate after he became furious at a waitress who spilled a drink on him during a meal. Although Ed did not spend an enormous amount of time monitoring his managers, he did want to get to know them very well before hiring them. If he hired quality managers with good character, he could trust them operating his businesses in various locations across the country. Ed was a fantastic recruiter and team builder. But that's only part of the equation. You also have to *develop* the talent you recruit.

I remember watching Jack Welch speak at GE one year. He was always passionate about hiring and retaining strong employees. I remember one statement he made, "The one great thing we did this year was hire a lot of smart people." Jack believed in churning the employee pool. He stressed that the top 10% performers should be promoted and rewarded financially. He also felt the bottom 10% should be fired. The middle 80% needed to be managed to improve their performance.

I always admired how vocal and painfully honest Jack Welch was when it came to managing employees. He spoke one time about managing to metrics (again discussed in detail later in the book) and segmenting your employee workforce by their ability to exhibit the values required by GE. He said the GE managers needed to divide their employees into 4 segments (note these are not meant to be equal in size):

1. Those that exhibit the GE values and reach their measured goals. These employees needed to be promoted or financially rewarded.
2. Those that exhibit the GE values but do not reach their measured goals. These employees needed to be given stretch goals and managed to meet those goals.
3. Those that do not exhibit the GE values and do not reach their measured goals. These employees needed to be fired.
4. Those that do not exhibit the GE values but make their measured goals. He took a few minutes to speak about this segment. It's been several years, so I'll paraphrase. He described this type of employee as, "The son of a bitch that makes the numbers, but stabs his peer in the back while doing it." He felt that these employees posed a great threat to the company and managers needed to keep a close eye on anyone that may fall into this segment.

GE Capital generally did a great job of developing their management staff. The company offered massive amounts of training and development opportunities, so we could not only learn and understand our specific job, but also broaden our educational base by learning other functional areas for stretch roles in the future. Managers up and down the chain of command generally did a great job of mentoring their subordinate managers. I was in both the mentor and protégé roles. As a Black Belt, I had a mentor that was the COO of the company. Organizationally, he was three management layers above me. It showed how committed the company was to getting us mentored by a high quality manager.

Even though the Army didn't have a formal mentor program, it had a very structured learning and development program for the commissioned officers. I was blessed to have so many great leaders to learn from at the early stages of my career. I also looked outside of my immediate surroundings for strong role models. In my early years in the Army I kept an eye on Lieutenant General William Pagonis, the mastermind behind the logistics of Desert Storm. He had recently retired and left the Army to take a leadership role at Sears Roebuck and Co. as Senior Vice President and Head of Supply Chain. I thought, "How will he handle managing in a corporate environment versus the military?" He was equally as successful at Sears as he was in the Army. He pledged not to waste his subordinate's time. One of the ways he honored this pledge was to have "stand-up meetings" in rooms with no chairs. This was an effective tool to keep the meetings brief and to the point. In the Army, he used pick up basketball games to get soldiers to open up and give him some "straight talk" about how things were going. At Sears he strongly encouraged his managers to play basketball with him as a tool to build teamwork and camaraderie.

After watching so many business owners, corporate managers, and military leaders succeed and fail in leading their operations, it is obvious that the successful ones understand how to recruit, manage and develop their junior leaders. Having a high IQ, being a strong individual contributor, and having a boatload of experience and institutional knowledge are all wonderful things. These things can give you a tremendous individual competitive advantage over your peers or competition. However, if you cannot effectively bring in good people, manage them, and develop them to help you run your operation over the long term, you will have a great deal of difficulty in exponentially growing your operation. The leaders that are unable to step away from the day to day operations to focus on the long-range goals and strategies are doomed for fatigue, burnout, and eventually failure. On the flip side, I've seen so many wealthy business leaders that owe their success to being good, not great mind you, but good at building and developing teams. If you can do this you give yourself a tremendous advantage at becoming successful.

Take Charge and Control Your Own Destiny

If you don't control your own destiny, someone else will do it for you. I witnessed many great leaders in the Army sit back and let an unknown personnel officer in Washington determine where their next critical job would be. The wrong assignment location or position could significantly help or hinder their career. Only a few of the officers I knew actually took aggressive steps to manage their career from a strategic level. It's really a shame, because so many good officers wound up leaving the military because of bad experiences they had at a duty assignment. Going to Korea may be one man's idea of a vacation, and yet it may be another man's idea of purgatory. I was amazed at watching sharp young men and women who would successfully lead large groups of soldiers through difficult situations, then sit back and lose control of their career when it came to upcoming assignments. Once I was in transition between units as a lieutenant. Before my file ended up on a personnel officer's desk, I went out and found the position I wanted and interviewed for it. This was practically unheard of in the military, at least for lower ranking officers. Knowing that I would someday need an impressive resume for corporate America, I pressed for an assignment that would help me with that aspect. On a personal vacation day I walked into the Battalion Executive Officer's office and told him I wanted to be part of his unit and more specifically I identified the platoon I wanted to lead. People didn't normally interview for a job in the Army, but he liked my moxie and picked up the phone. Within days the paperwork was moving for my transfer. I constantly saw other officers that just waited for orders to come down. Some went to Korea, Iraq, Kuwait, or other hard duty assignments. These are life changing events that affected the officers and their families. I was amazed that my peers just accepted them without trying to influence their future job assignments at all!

The same holds true for corporate careers. I've seen solid leaders just accept the positions that are laid out by their managers. The most frequent problem was the managers would usually assume their subordinates wanted to stay at the local office. The leaders that expanded their horizons and considered a larger array of jobs at a variety of locations and an assortment of external companies consistently moved up the ladder faster.

One other thing I noticed with corporate career development was the greener grass syndrome. I was amazed at how companies tended to give too much credence to external candidates. I consistently saw companies pass over well qualified internal candidates to bring in an external candidate that was equally or slightly less qualified. Another spin on this syndrome was the pay scale. I saw quite a few situations that would pan out like this. A good manager would follow a career path and get a promotion within her company. An equally good manager would follow the same career path and then leave to take a promotion with an external company. Each manager would continue to get promoted and the one that left eventually came back to the original company. There they were, working side by side on the same level and with the same company. Which one wound up with the higher pay? The one that left and came back. Many of the managers I worked with just accepted it as an unwritten rule.

Those people that raced up the corporate ladder or exponentially expanded their own business also tended to be great at selling themselves. The cold hard truth is if you can't sell yourself, you're going to have a tough time selling your product or service. Even if you're not in sales, you have to pitch ideas to peers, senior managers, executives, business owners, etc. Interviewing for higher paying jobs, pitching your services as a consultant, and pitching your company to a potential customer all require the need to sell yourself. One common technique used to sell is the elevator speech. This speech gets its name from its use. When a colleague, manager, or influencer is in the elevator with you, there is usually a time period of 60 seconds or so during which you share the ride. This elevator ride provides a golden opportunity to give a short pitch on anything you're selling. It can be anything from a project you want to get pushed through to a job promotion you've applied for. Of course it's not just limited to brief encounters in elevators. I have used these with my Black Belt projects, selling real estate investments, selling my company's services in real estate, and when asking for a promotion. Many of the successful people I know use techniques like this to not only to sell a product or service, but also to sell themselves and accelerate their career.

One of the best pieces of advice my father ever gave me was the notion that nothing is impossible if you set your mind to it. Successful people don't go along with the status quo just because everyone else does. Set your goals and make a plan on how you will achieve them. Once you set your long-term goals, strategically plan what is necessary in order to achieve those goals. Next, set short term goals that support the long-term ones. Finally, set up a way to manage your progress. If you don't, you will be adrift without a compass.

Building and Managing Your Business

"It's not the employer who pays the wages. Employers only handle the money. It's the customer who pays the wages." - Henry Ford

Strategic planning and managing through metrics are both critical for building and managing your business. The term metrics is defined as a standard of measurement. I remember the first time

I heard the word metrics. I was in my first week at GE and my mentor, TJ Webb, was giving me a crash course on corporate America, GE Capital, and the leasing industry. I was very fortunate. TJ was a former Army officer who also transitioned straight from the military to GE. We were tank platoon leaders in the same company and had been good friends for years. He was generous enough to get me interviews with both the head of quality and the head of operations for the company. I once heard, "What you know is important, but who you know is critical!" That thought certainly resonated with me when I was out looking for my first job outside of the military.

In any event, I'm in a conference room drinking from a fire hose as my old friend TJ is throwing all the new acronyms at me and trying to get me to shift my mindset from military to corporate. There were a lot of similarities on the leadership side such as focusing on the objective or end state, inspiring others to accomplish a mission, setting the standard or example, leading from the front, delegating, empowering, etc. However, the Army was different in some ways such as monitoring productivity and overtime, two related topics. The military was unique in that man hours were flexible. If we needed to stay late, we did. Overtime was not in the Army's vocabulary. While we were under budget constraints in the military, it was a secondary focus. While it was negatively viewed to go over budget, we were never rewarded for coming in under budget. Abusing soldiers' time and overworking them was a practice that was not tolerated. At the same time, there was rarely a reward for being overly productive and finishing early. I now needed to learn how to think in terms of productivity and measurements of productivity. GE measured productivity down to the lowest possible element. They used metrics to assist in managing processes and employees. Their Six Sigma Black Belts and greenbelts used metrics to drive out variation and increase productivity. Sure, we had some basic metrics that we used in the Army, but at GE they were fanatical about it.

As I mentioned earlier in the book, GE uses the acronym CTQ, which stands for Critical To Quality. It refers to what the customer's needs are. When a process output does not meet the customer CTQ, it is called a defect. Great companies take the time to measure their performance relative to customer CTQs. Top performing managers do this religiously. They understand what their customer CTQs are, understand where they are performing relative to their customer CTQs, and utilize metrics to manage the process.

GE drove the use of metrics down to the lowest possible level. At the leasing company I worked at we had several of our metrics in real time. For example, we could look up on a board and see how many customers were waiting on hold and how many had been waiting past the acceptable time limit. We could go on our intranet and view the number of customers on the phone or in queue to speak with each representative as they went through the interactive voice response system. We used metrics to benchmark where we were historically with a process, and then we would design projects around improving specific metrics (decreasing customer wait times, increasing customer satisfaction, reducing expenses, etc.). After the project was complete we measured our success by the corresponding increase or decrease in the associated metrics.

I remember working with a young sharp lieutenant when I was on a brigadier general's staff in Saudi Arabia. Most of the senior officers back then could barely use a computer. This kid came in with a strong knowledge and understanding of developing spreadsheets and graphs. He looked around our operation and realized that the senior officers occasionally received sparse reports on the budget, sometimes hand written. As the budget officer, he jumped on the opportunity to standardize all the reporting. When asked how their operation was performing according to planned budget or how they compared to last year's budget, a senior officer would probably have dug through reams of paper files to find the numbers. Now they could have graphs and visual aids to better understand the various expense accounts and it was all stored on a central computer and updated daily. The graphs he produced really helped everyone better understand the expenses. Sometimes it's difficult to see the trees through the forest, especially when it comes to volumes of numbers. He took reports that looked like this:

SAMPLE: ANNUAL BUDGET TRANS & CONTRACTS

Total	$74,200,000
Ammunition	$ 5,436,000
Equipment	$64,769,000
Food	$ 795,000
Fuel	$ 3,200,000

SAMPLE: ANNUAL BUDGET EQUIPMENT

Equipment	$64,769,000
Aircraft, Fixed Wing	$28,500,000
Aircraft, Rotary Wing	$12,429,000
Clothing	$ 1,387,000
Communications	$ 4,238,000
Navigational Aids	$ 789,000
Nuclear, Biological, Chemical	$ 994,000
Repair Parts	$ 6,289,000
Track Vehicles	$ 7,853,000
Wheeled Vehicles	$ 2,200,000

Then he transformed it into a user friendly format like this:

Equipment	$ 64,769,000
Ammunition	$ 5,436,000
Fuel	$ 3,200,000
Food	$ 795,000
Total	$ 74,200,000

EQUIPMENT		
Aircraft - Fixed Wing	$	28,500,000
Aircraft - Rotary Wing	$	12,429,000
Track Vehicles	$	7,853,000
Repair Parts	$	6,289,000
Communications	$	4,328,000
Wheeled Vehicles	$	2,200,000
Clothing	$	1,387,000
Nuclear Biological Chemical	$	994,000
Navigational Aids	$	789,000
Total	$	64,769,000

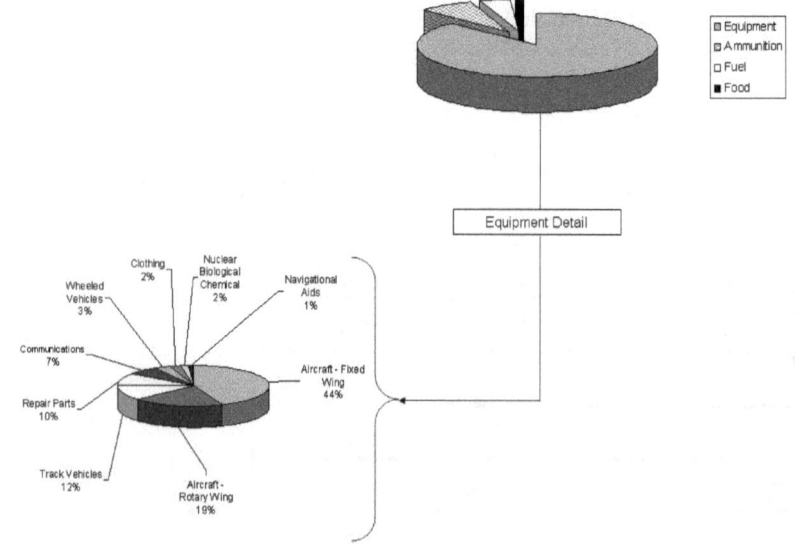

When the senior officers had to explain their expenses over the last year, they would often have to dig into hard copies of expense reports. In turn, their report would look something like this:

	Annual	Q1 Actual	Q1 Budget	Q2 Actual
Equipment	$ 64,769,000	$ 31,258,000	$ 25,907,600	$ 17,159,000
Ammunition	$ 5,436,000	$ 1,900,000	$ 2,174,400	$ 1,147,000
Fuel	$ 3,200,000	$ 1,030,000	$ 1,280,000	$ 957,000
Food	$ 795,000	$ 201,000	$ 318,000	$ 194,000
Total	$ 74,200,000	$ 34,389,000	$ 29,680,000	$ 19,457,000

Q2 Budget	Q3 Actual	Q3 Budget	Available for Q4	Q4 Budget
$ 16,192,250	$ 12,462,000	$ 12,953,800	$ 3,890,000	$ 9,715,350
$ 1,359,000	$ 1,069,000	$ 1,087,200	$ 1,320,000	$ 815,400
$ 800,000	$ 1,105,000	$ 640,000	$ 108,000	$ 480,000
$ 198,750	$ 203,000	$ 159,000	$ 197,000	$ 119,250
$18,550,000	$ 14,839,000	$ 14,840,000	$ 5,515,000	$ 11,130,000

Our lieutenant took the data and created a chart, enabling everyone to visualize it and thus making it more user friendly. Here's an example using the Equipment category:

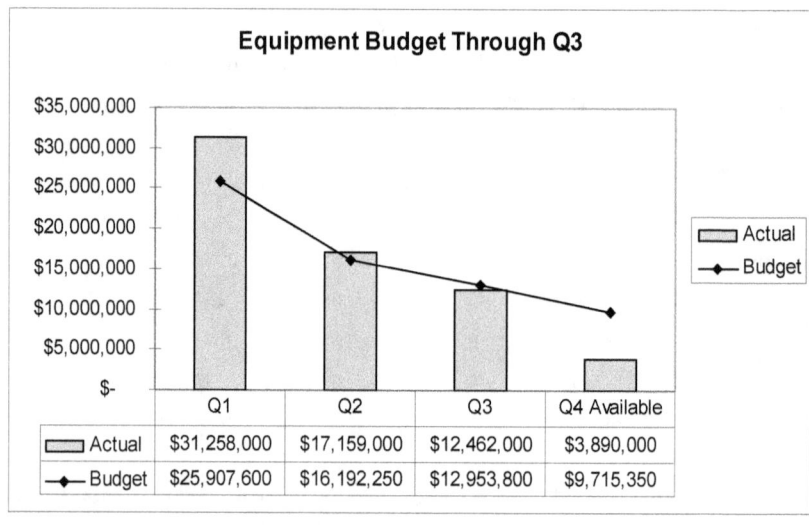

Equipment Budget Through Q3

	Q1	Q2	Q3	Q4 Available
Actual	$31,258,000	$17,159,000	$12,462,000	$3,890,000
Budget	$25,907,600	$16,192,250	$12,953,800	$9,715,350

Voila! The kid was everybody's new best friend!

Many business owners and managers find themselves drowning in debt. It's easy to get overwhelmed with all the bills coming in monthly. Some people lose perspective on how much is going out in accounts payable. They can't see the forest through the trees! The successful managers can take a step back and look at the situation strategically. They can track expenses, visualize the data, and initiate strategic cost-cutting initiatives based on what they see in the data. A chart like the one used by the lieutenant is a great way to visualize the data and better understand it. Successful managers use charts like this to quickly identify necessary and unnecessary spending and cut costs accordingly.

The successful business managers and business owners I watched over the years at a minimum kept metrics of the items affecting cash flow: income and expenses. From the behemoth that is GE to the mom and pop corner store, every successful business owner or manager that was responsible for the profit and loss of the company kept a tight reign on income and expenses. That's what it all boils down to eventually. The strong companies that were vaulting over their competition were constantly refocusing on increasing sales and driving down expenses.

The use of metrics feeds into strategic planning. Imagine a company without *any* sales goals. Imagine a company without *realistic* sales goals. How about a company that has sales goals, but does nothing to adjust strategy when they start to miss their goals? This really happens. I've seen people start companies without pro-forma income or cash flow statements. That is to say, they didn't take the time to anticipate what their income, expense and cash flow would be over the start-up period. Taking a few hours to research and estimate realistic expenses and revenues for a small or large business is not only smart, but essential. Here is a basic example. As simple as this seems, I've seen people invest hundreds of thousands of dollars without conducting the research to create something as basic as this.

Sample Pro Forma Income Statement Fro Boutique Retail Store
Jan 1 to Dec 31

INCOME

Gross Sales	$750,000	
Less Returns & Allowances	$ 1,000	
Equals Net Sales		$749,000
Cost of Goods		
Inventory Jan 1	$345,000	
Plus Purchases	$220,000	
Plus Shipping Charges	$ 4,000	
Equals Total Inventory Cost	$569,000	
Less Inventory Value Dec 31	$200,000	
Equals Cost of Goods Sold		$369,000
Gross Profit (Net Sales – COGS)		$380,000
Interest Income	$ 1,000	
TOTAL INCOME		**$381,000**

EXPENSES

Payroll	$125,000	
Utilities	$ 4,000	
Rent	$ 29,000	
Insurance	$ 4,500	
Shipping	$ 12,000	
Office Supplies	$ 3,000	
Telephone	$ 4,000	
Interest Paid	$ 500	
Repairs & Maintenance	$ 2,000	
Equipment	$ 7,500	
TOTAL EXPENSES		**$191,500**
NET INCOME (Tot Inc – Tot Exp)		**$189,500**

Investing money blindly without conducting the proper due
diligence is like going into a fight with one hand tied behind your
back. The worst thing is they did this to themselves. I've
watched large companies with business development managers,
responsible for bringing in new strategic clients, who set
unrealistic sales goals because there was no real strategic

planning or analysis on how the company was going to achieve those goals. I've worked with so many small business owners that thought, "Well, I'm going to capture just a small percent of this multi-million dollar market. How hard can that be?" They would just jump right into their business without a clue of how long it may take to ramp up operations. They had no real idea of what it would take to staff or support a sales team to achieve those sales goals. What's equally bad is watching a company set goals, then do nothing month after month to strategically or tactically adjust for missing their goals. All of these businesses were ultimately doomed for failure.

I remember one of the best tools for planning and organizing my day was from a military leadership book I read as a young officer. It recommended writing down all the tasks I had to complete that day on a piece of paper (this predated common use of laptops & PDAs). Next, take the list and prioritize the tasks. Any tasks I did not complete by the end of the day should be included on the next day's list. This simple exercise has saved me an enormous amount of time over the years. I still do this exercise to this day, just not on paper! As simple as this exercise seems, you can follow a similar approach and use this for planning your business strategy.

The successful company leaders have a plan. They go through formal processes like the one above to develop the critical list of business strategies. Without going through these formal processes, a business can get stuck in a rut and fall behind the competition. Developing and adjusting your strategy can keep you competitive in the marketplace. One of the tools successful business owners and managers use is a SWOT. This is a process of analyzing their strengths, weaknesses, opportunities, and threats. Here is an actual SWOT used for a catalog flower company as they tried to transition to an internet flower company in the late 1990s.

SWOT for Internet Flower Company

STRENGTH
Industry leader
High margin by cutting out storefront/middleman
Provides perishable item to consumer quicker than competition
Strong relationship with FedEx
Relatively low fixed costs
CEO has strong marketing network with Time Magazine, Wall
Street Journal & others
Offer demand forecast with growers
No inventory

WEAKNESS
Reliant on growers – difficult to conduct quality check unless
order flowers yourself
Reliant on FedEx or other delivery service
New brand
Easily duplicated
Customers need a catalog or internet access to order
Initial impression to customer is poor – delivered in a box
Product is perishable
Unproven company

OPPORTUNITY
Potential market overseas in Europe
Offer strong relationship with growers – help level sales in their
seasonal business
Sunday deliveries through couriers offer opening into large
market share (traditional storefronts closed on Sundays)
Potential to expand market share with upscale retailers

THREAT
Grocery stores increasing market share
Growing competition within internet
FTD pushing internet sales

Recommendations:
Tap into the Sunday delivery market.
CEO offers marketing network and experience needed to push
into upscale retailer market.

This company not only penetrated the Sunday delivery market
and in early 2010 was known as one of the best luxury online
florists, but they also successfully entered into the European
market.

Successful company leaders also envision an end state. That is to
say, they foresee what the successful business will look, feel and
act like in the future when it is running at capacity. They lay out
Mission, Vision and Values statements. They "backwards plan"
by understanding what their company should be doing ultimately
to be successful, then they strategically develop a plan to get to
that state of success. They develop reasonable and obtainable
sales goals and anticipate expenses using techniques like
analyzing industry data, obtaining vendor quotes, and scouting
their competition, and then they develop strategic plans of how to
obtain those goals. Once annual sales and expense goals are
obtained, they are further segmented into quarterly, monthly and
sometimes weekly or even daily goals. These are not simply
derived by dividing the annual goal by 12 to get the monthly
goal. Successful leaders consider industry trends, production
schedules, logistical limitations, product roll-outs, customer
demand, and a host of other industry specific variables to predict
sales and expense figures, and in turn develop goals from that
data.

Here is a sample sales forecast for a retail store selling children's
clothing:

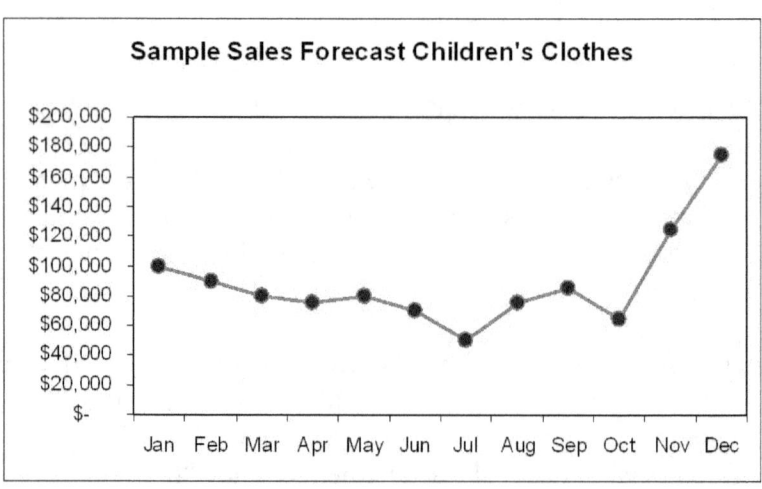

Again, I've seen people buy or open businesses without even having some sales forecasts as basic as this. This forecast should be based on past performance, and then adjusted for any variables that will affect the sales cycle. Our example shows a remodeling project affecting the shopping center and a corresponding drop in sales over the summer. Basic metrics such as this can be an enormous tool for the business manager or owner. The next step is to break the store sales projections down into department projections. Department projections can be broken down into team projections. As they progress through the year, actual sales data can be compared to the projected figures. Comparing the two can be insightful. Do the projected figures fall short of the actual sales? Do they exceed actual sales? How accurate are the projections? If they are not accurate, is it because the projections are not realistic, or is it because of problems with the sales process? This is just the tip of the iceberg. The successful managers and owners I dealt with made good use of critical metrics. When used correctly and judiciously, they can be a strong and useful tool for managing business operations.

PART II
SIX SIGMA

Why bring the subject of Six Sigma up in a personal finance book? So many wealthy people I know utilize Six Sigma without even knowing it. Some use metrics to measure processes. Some use sampling techniques for quality control. Some use data analysis to identify weaknesses in processes. Others use best practice techniques when trying to develop or enhance a process. The bottom line is lots of people utilize Six Sigma tools on a daily basis without ever knowing it. In fact, many of these people may have never even heard the term Six Sigma and therefore have no idea that they are using Six Sigma tools in their day to day operations. My intent is to share some of the basic and common Six Sigma tools with you. These tools are the same ones used over and over by successful business owners and managers, and they can help you not only shave your expenses, but also increase your revenue.

This is a great time to delve into Six Sigma because it dovetails well with the metrics topic. Six Sigma is a process improvement program used by GE and many other fortune 500 companies. It is a powerful and robust tool that is often used to increase productivity and efficiency. In a nutshell, it is a statistically based methodology that often requires leading project teams to drive out variation and decrease the number of defects occurring in a process. Imagine an aircraft manufacturer like Boeing that needs to produce 350 B-737 aircraft this year. Suppose that during the final assembly of the aircraft, they have a quality control check which reveals 20 planes per year with one or more problems that need to be addressed. That sounds pretty innocuous at first glance. But consider that each plane with a problem needs a team to address the issue, or worst case holds up production for the rest of the assembly line. The process of slowing or stopping production to go back and fix a product that should have been produced correctly the first time is devastating to manufacturers. It requires additional labor, overhead, transportation, equipment, parts – the list goes on. It's not a stretch to think this could cause millions of dollars a day in expenses just for this one line of aircraft. Enter Six Sigma. By implementing a process improvement process such as Six Sigma, reducing the number of defects by 20% or so can add millions to this company's bottom line.

A lot of people say that Six Sigma is only viable with manufacturing processes. Consider another example that's from a finance company. The company I worked for, VFS, was a division of GE Capital. Our company had a goal of having our customer's payments applied to our bank account within four days of the customer putting it in the mail. The time between the customer placing the check in the mail and the payment being applied to our account was referred to as "float time." We worked with the bank as well as several of other companies within GE Capital. We ultimately leveraged some great ideas from one of our sister companies that had already gone through some projects on reducing float time. This enabled us to decrease our float time by half of a day and in turn generate hundreds of thousands of dollars annually in interest from the funds. My goal as a Six Sigma Black Belt at GE was to save the company a minimum of $1,000,000 per year.

Six Sigma isn't just about reducing defects. It's also geared toward completely satisfying the customer's needs. These two goals, reducing defects and satisfying customer's needs, are two sides of the same coin. The link between the two is the fact that defects should be based off of your customer needs. For example, if the customer needs an aircraft part delivered within 24 hours of ordering it, any parts arriving after 24 hours should be flagged as a defect. What if you don't utilize Six Sigma or some similar type of quality program? What if you ignore your customer's concerns? Eventually you will lose the customer. Imagine the costs associated with replacing a customer. You have the business development side that has to seek out a new customer. You have the integration side that needs to handle the absorption of the new customer. You have the sales side that needs to adapt to meeting the new customer's needs. Finally you have the operations side that needs to adapt to supporting the new customer. It is tremendously expensive to replace customers as opposed to keeping your current customers. Six Sigma allows a business of any size to refocus on the customer's needs or develop ways to focus on those needs if there was no previously existing platform.

The process of becoming a certified Six Sigma Black Belt is tedious and can take over a year, even if you're working at it full time. Many of the successful managers and business owners I've worked with used some of the more common sense oriented Six Sigma tools while running their operations. Here are some of the tools which they utilized to run their businesses more efficiently. They are outlined in what is called the DMAIC process, which stands for Define, Measure, Analyze, Improve and Control.

Define the Process

When undertaking a Six Sigma project, you first define the scope of work involved and gain an understanding of the process. Great managers understand who their customers are, what their customer CTQs (Critical to Quality) are, and what defects are. While the majority of customers lie outside of the organization, don't forget the internal customers. The human resources department, for example, serves the internal employees and therefore should treat them as customers. The best business managers I know are fanatical about customer centricity. They always focus on what the customer requirements are and they understand that their requirements change over time. What may be considered a delighter today may be considered a requirement tomorrow. When remote controls first came out for televisions, they were delighters. The customer didn't expect them on every model, just the high end ones. Today, selling a television without a remote is inconceivable. The customers of the market have come to expect them with even the lowest grade models. Great companies understand their customer's CTQs as well as their delighters. They realize that they must first understand their customer's expectations before they can start delighting them. Once the CTQs are understood, you can measure defects. A defect is something that does not meet the customer CTQ. Once you can measure your defects, you can manage them through the use of metrics. Here's an example:

Voice of the Customer: "It's great when I can get my pizza delivered within 20 minutes, but I really expect it within 30 minutes."
Customer CTQ: "I want my pizza delivered to my house in ½ hour or less."
Defect: Any pizza not delivered to customer within 30 minutes.
Delighter: Any pizza delivered within 20 minutes or less.

Process Mapping

Similar to the way they utilize metrics; successful managers _visualize_ the process by mapping or blueprinting it out. Memorializing a process in this manner assists with things like training new employees and process improvement initiatives. It generally helps in organizing and understanding processes. Here's an example of a process map:

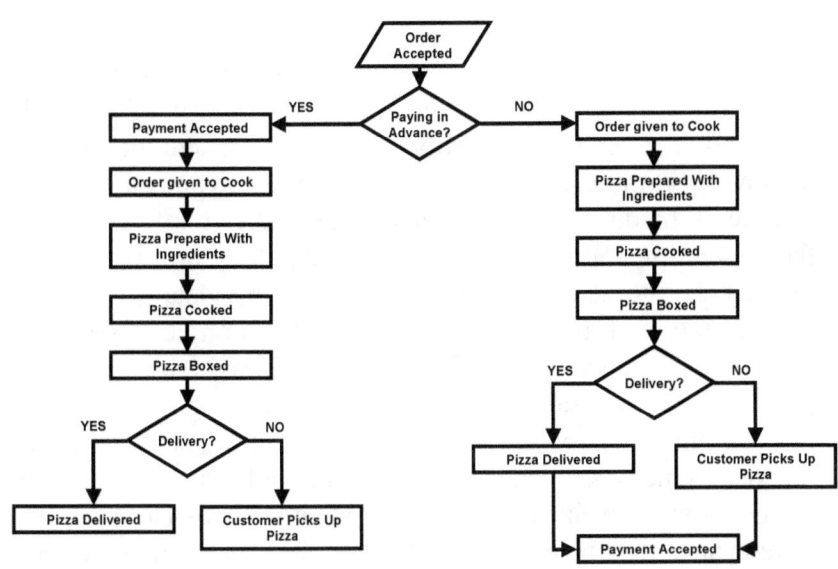

While defining the process it's also a good idea to estimate the benefits a Six Sigma project will provide. A good initial financial estimate of the benefits can go a long way in determining if a project is worth the time to undertake. Not *all* CTQs of *every* customer can be met *every* time.[6]

Measure

As I stated previously, my friend, Jimmy, who owns a portfolio of gas stations / convenience stores built a predictive model to forecast revenues of other stores. He can use this model to analyze a store he wants to acquire or build. The model can also be used to estimate the value of a target store. He was able to build this model by first measuring the data he had at all of the stores he owned. Jimmy understands the value of measuring performance and putting that information to work for his benefit.

Understanding your key processes and measuring them is critical. When you look at a process, you are looking at a set of data. The entire set is called the population. It is often difficult or costly to look at the entire set of data. If this is the case, you can take a sample of the data and from that sample, make an inference about the population. Whether you are gathering data from your external or internal customers, be sure to gather data representative of the entire population. For example, if your company bakes a variety of donuts and utilizes three work shifts per day, don't just sample donuts from the third shift. And don't just sample the chocolate frosted ones. Be sure your sample size touches as many shifts and segments of donuts as possible. The larger the sample size the more accurate it will be. However, the sample size must be economically feasible. Taking a bite out of every donut made might not be the best business practice!

Donuts Produced in October
(Population)

	Chocolate Frosted	Cake	Frosted
Shift 1	1200	500	2000
Shift 2	1650	750	2000
Shift 3	1700	1000	2000

Donuts Sampled in October

	Chocolate Frosted	Cake	Frosted
Shift 1	60	25	100
Shift 2	83	38	100
Shift 3	85	50	100

When you think about measuring a process, it's important to understand the critical parts of the process to measure. A simple tool called the cause and effect diagram can assist in determining those critical parts of the process to measure. Here's an example of a cause and effect diagram.

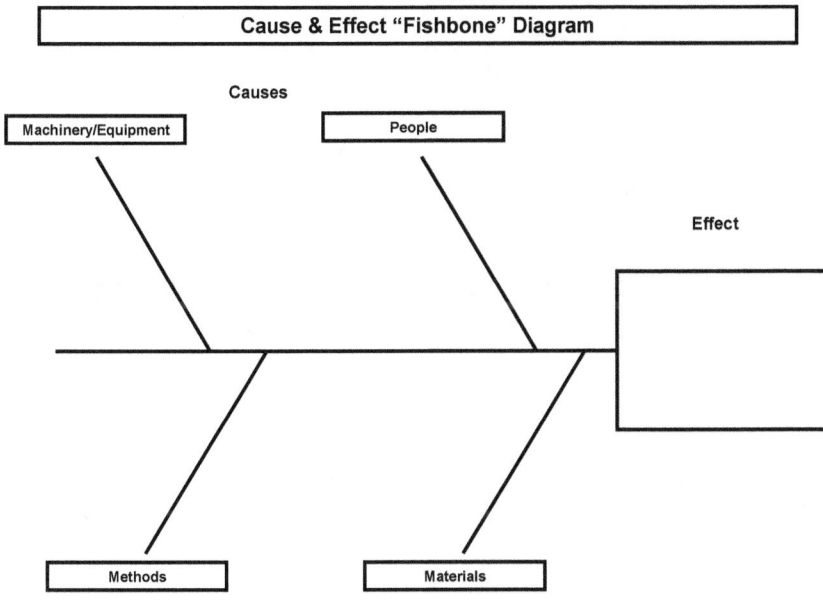

Let's say you're not meeting one of your customer CTQs and you want to understand why. The cause and effect diagram is a tool used to identify the most likely causes for not meeting the CTQ. The cause and effect diagram helps to *visualize* your process in terms of inputs and outputs. The input variables all affect the output. You simply ask "why?" Why is the pizza delivered late to the customer? The answers to that question are the inputs to the process. Once you understand the major input variables, you place them on the chart.

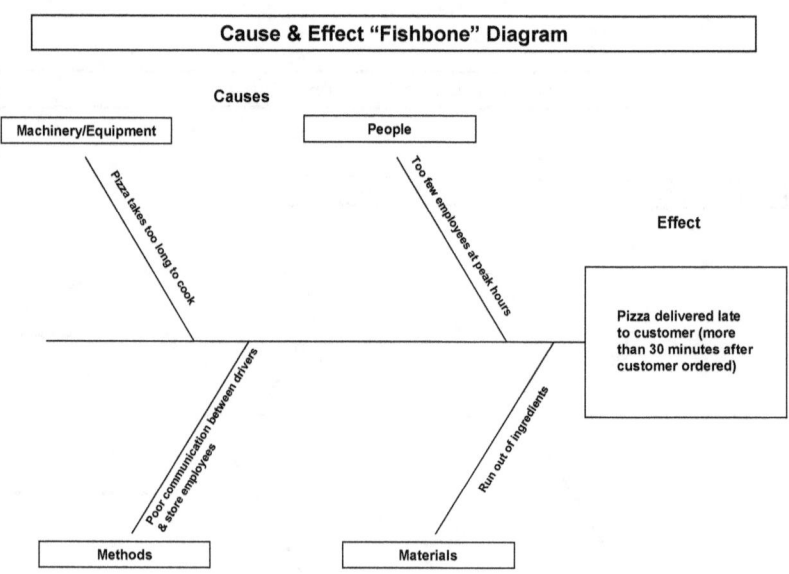

From here, you drill down on each input variable, asking "why?" Why does the pizza take too long to cook? Keep asking "why" until you've identified all critical input variables in the process. Now you have the critical inputs identified and can start measuring the process.

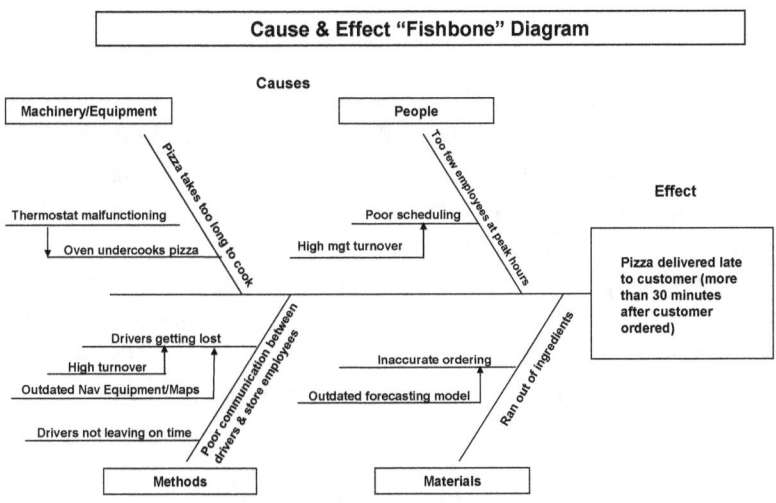

Displaying variation

Display data in the form of metrics. Am I beating a dead hose here? I just can't tell you how many successful CEOs, CFOs, executives, and millionaire business owners I have seen in action managing through metrics. They spend _volumes_ of time managing by metrics. When the expectations are not meshing with the results, they perform a gap analysis to understand why company performance is not meeting expectations. Ultimately they devise a plan and execute solutions to decrease the gap. Before they devise a plan to improve the performance, they must analyze the data. And in order to analyze it, you should display it in a way that is readily understood.

Almost every repetitive process has variation. Variation is the spread or dispersion of the data. When you start your computer or automobile, does it take the _exact_ same amount of time to start *every* time? Of course not. If you start your computer 50 days in a row and measure the amount of time it takes to start, the difference between the slowest time and the fastest time is the variation. Generally speaking, excessive variation is bad for a process because it represents inconsistency. Would you be happy if your car started within 1-3 seconds every time you tried to start it? Probably so. Would you be equally satisfied if 1 out of every 5 times it took 1 full minute to start? Absolutely not. The histogram is a popular tool to look at data over a period of time and gives a great picture of the process. It provides a look at the variation, shape and center of the data. Let's look at the pizzeria example and display some data in the form of a histogram.

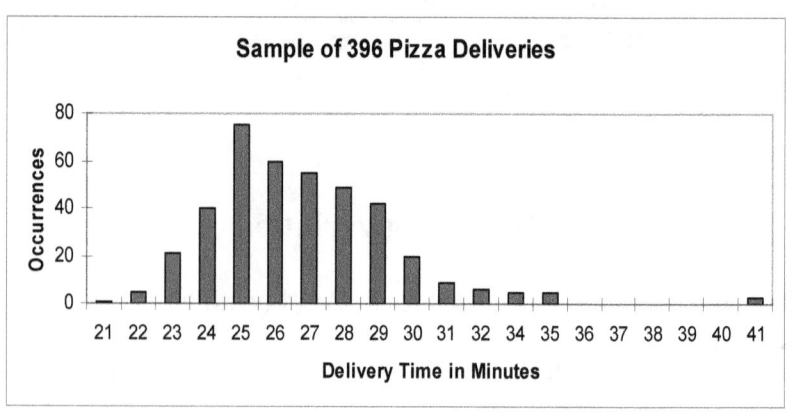

This histogram gives us a picture of the data. You can understand quite a bit about the process by looking at this display of data. One thing the histogram is useful for is showing the central tendency of the data. Just glancing at the histogram, you can see the most frequent delivery time was 25 minutes. You can conduct some basic calculations and better understand the central tendency by calculating the mean, median and mode. The mean is the average of all the delivery times. The median is the middle of the data set (where 50% of the data is greater than the median and 50% is less than the median). The mode is the most frequently occurring number. The mean, median and mode coincide with our visual observation.

Mean: 26.8
Median: 26
Mode: 25

What else can you glean from this picture of data? Let's take a step back and consider the process, along with the customer's CTQ while we look at the data. What's the customer's CTQ? The customer wants the pizza delivered within 30 minutes. That gives you what's called an upper specification limit (USL). It's the upper limit allowable for the process to meet the customer CTQ. Many processes also have a lower specification limit (LSL). A good example of a product designed with both a USL and an LSL would be the diameter of an aircraft propeller shaft that spins at several thousand revolutions per minute. The manufacturer has to ensure the diameter of each shaft falls within the prescribed limits. One millimeter too large or small could cause catastrophic failure for the aircraft. If you overlay the USL to the pizza delivery histogram, you will see where the defects are, along with the unsatisfied customers.

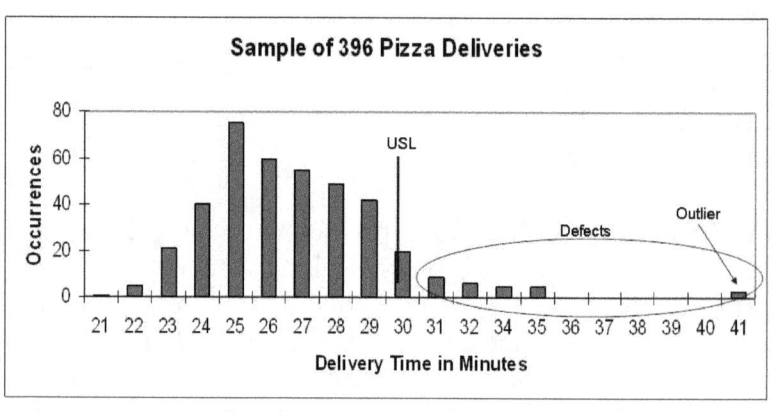

The fantastic thing about the histogram is being able to see the process. Just by looking at this data you can ascertain that, as the process currently stands, it takes X amount of minutes to make the pizza and Y amount of time to deliver them. You can assume there are a handful of customers that are located very close to the store and they receive their deliveries quickly. Another fair assumption is there are some customers on the outer edge of the delivery area that take longer to get to. The bulk of the customers are serviced in time, with a few receiving their pizza after 30 minutes – these are the defects and they should be resolved. One other interesting point this graph shows is the outlier at the far right. There were three deliveries that took 41 minutes to deliver. An outlier is a data point that lies abnormally far away from the rest of the data population. It is important to understand and resolve outliers. Does this display an error in the way they timed the deliveries while collecting the delivery times? Did these three deliveries take place on the same day? Were they associated with the same driver? Were there problems with the internal processes (i.e. the oven, scheduling, etc.) during these defects? Or is this simply a group of customers that are located far away from the store? It is critical to identify and eliminate outliers.

Once you identify, understand and eliminate the outliers from the process, it's time to focus on the rest of the defects. With this data set, there are three approaches to attack the defects while proceeding through the DMAIC process. The first approach is to reduce variation, and "tighten" the process by bringing the delivery times closer to the mean. That would give us a shift from this:

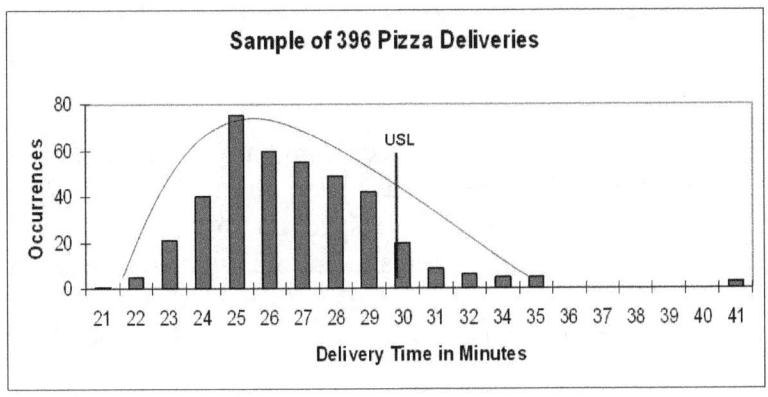

To a histogram looking more like this:

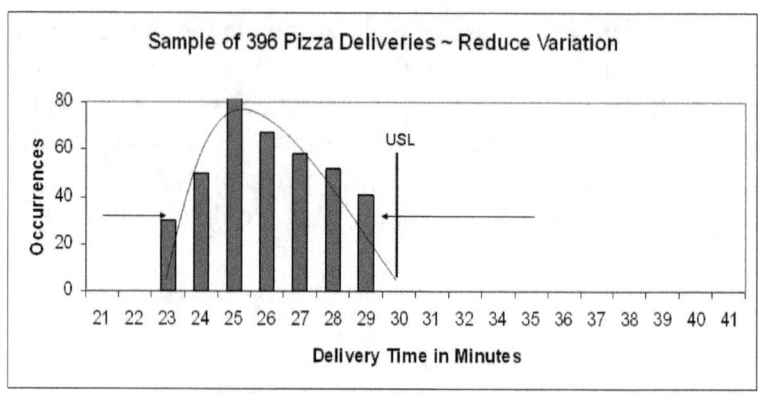

Sample of 396 Pizza Deliveries ~ Reduce Variation

You can see the outliers have been eliminated, and the longest delivery times of 35 minutes have been trimmed down to 29 minutes. On the other end of the spectrum, the shortest delivery times of 21 minutes have been shifted to 23 minutes. This shows a process with relatively more mass in the central area. This means it's a process with less variation and more predictability.

The second approach is to shift the entire process, along with the mean, to the left of the USL. After identifying and eliminating the outliers, you would reduce the delivery time across the board shifting the histogram from this:

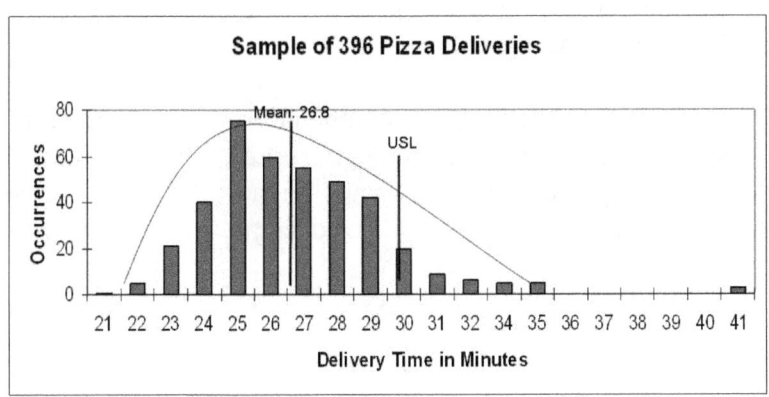

To this:

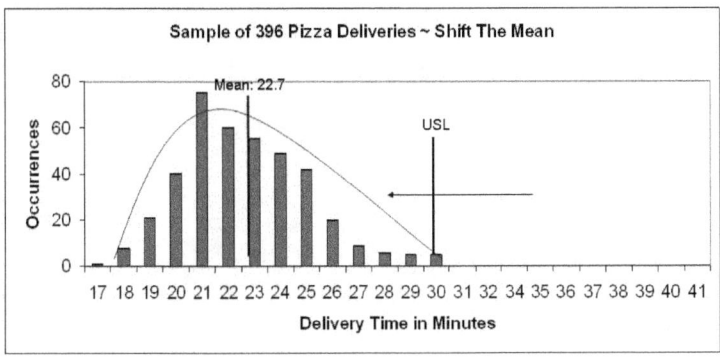

You can see the longest delivery time has shifted from 35 minutes to 30 minutes. The shortest times have also shifted from

21 minutes to 17 minutes. The mean delivery time has shifted from 26.8 minutes to 22.7. The variation has not been affected, but the late deliveries (defects) have been eliminated by shortening the entire process.

The third approach is simply a combination of reducing variation and shifting the mean. This is the most preferable; as it combines the strengths of the previous two approaches. You can see the reduction of the mean as well as the decrease in variation from this:

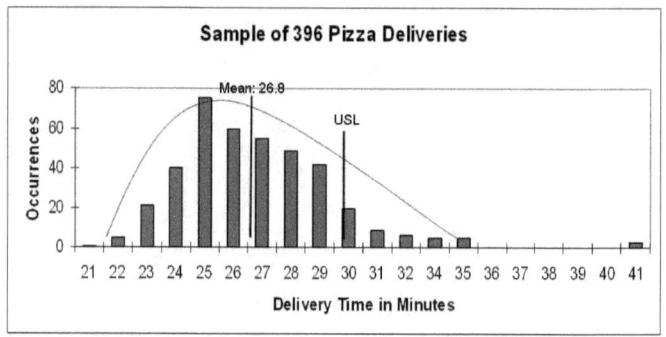

To this:

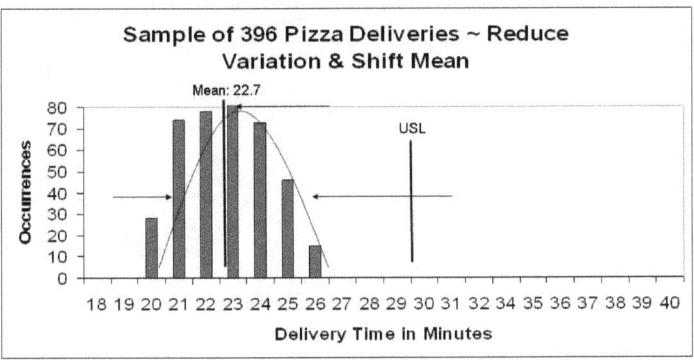

Another recommendation for measuring the process is gaining an understanding of the data across time. The run chart is a good tool to measure changes over time. On the next page is an example of a run chart. Notice there is a noticeable upward "shift" in the delivery times sampled on the 14th of the month for the 1st shift of employees, while the 2nd shift of employees seem to have less variation in their delivery times. The run chart can also be used to baseline your process. Once you've established a baseline, after you make any changes to the process you can compare it to the baseline and understand any improvements made.

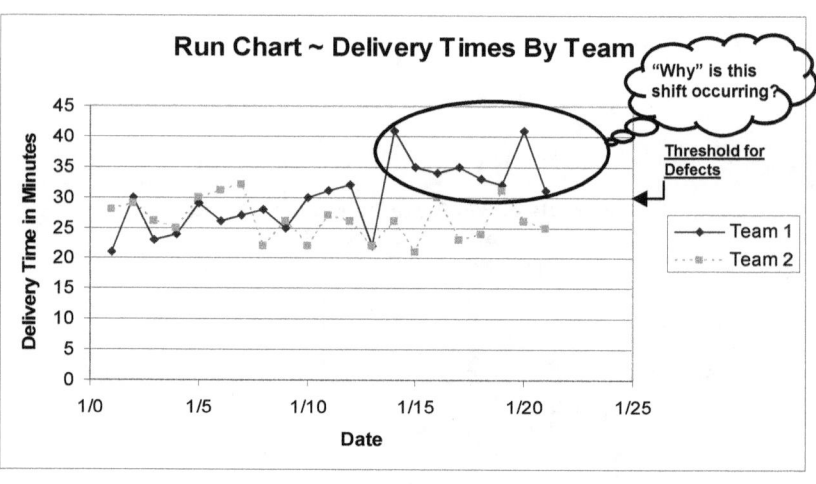

The run chart just reviewed can also be a good tool to measure defects over time. The LSL or USL (in this case the 30 minute mark) indicates the threshold for defects.

During the measure phase you need to identify, measure, and determine the root cause for your defects. You should investigate any defects and determine the root cause for future improvements. The Pareto chart is a good tool for this. Similar to the way the lieutenant identified and ranked the expenses from highest to lowest visually, the Pareto chart can be a great tool to identify the critical defects that are causing the majority of the problems. The Pareto chart is named after Vilfredo Pareto, a 19th century economist. The chart stems from the Pareto Principle which states that 80% of the problems come from 20% of the causes. The idea is that you can focus on making a few critical improvements to just a small portion of the process and deliver big results. Here's an example of a Pareto chart:

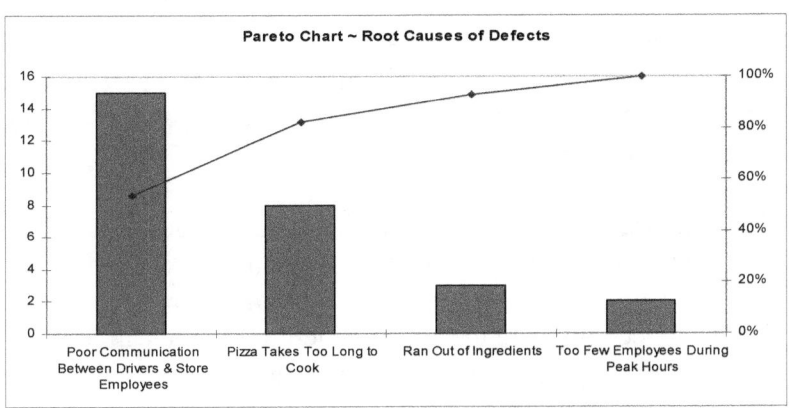

You can further drill down into the sub-processes of "Poor Communication Between Drivers & Store Employees" to uncover the root causes, as shown below.

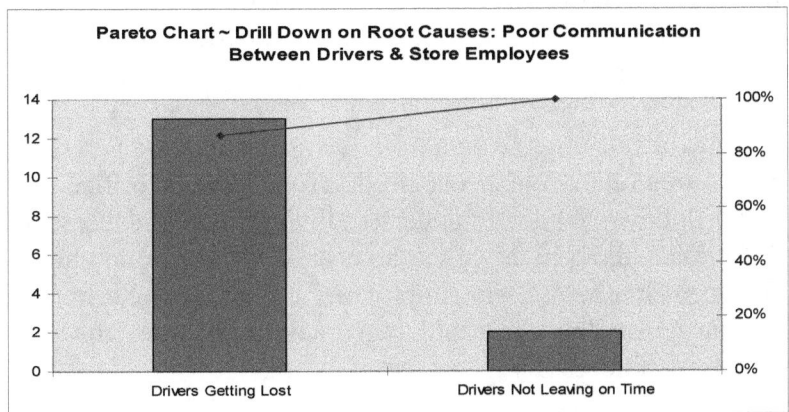

It's easy to see how the Pareto chart can be used hand in hand with the cause and effect diagram. Just keep asking "why" and drill down to the root causes of your defects. The Pareto chart simply helps you visualize the results and focus on the critical problems within the process.

The measure phase is all about understanding your processes in relation to your customer CTQs, identifying the key inputs to your processes, and measuring your output as it relates to your CTQs. Once you have these items identified, you can measure them and display the data. Measuring data is a fine balance. You can't measure everything, so be judicious with the samples you take. On the other hand, it's a lot easier to measure as many processes and sub processes as you can the first time. Going back a second or third time to measure a process after the fact can be painful and time consuming.[7]

Analyze

During the analyze phase you want to identify a list of possible causes for the defects, narrow the list to the root causes, and quantify the benefits.

Start by identifying the data from the measure phase where the most variation or defects occurred. From there, prioritize the list and drill down to gain an understanding of the root causes for the defects (i.e. the drill down Pareto chart on "Poor Communication Between Drivers & Store Employees"). This may require more measuring, so don't be afraid to go back to measure sub-processes if necessary.

Finally you want to quantify the benefits by determining the cost of the new process (with the defects removed). Compare this to the original cost of the process with the defects in place and you have your financial benefit. If the benefit doesn't outweigh the cost, then the project isn't worth completing and you need to reevaluate the scope and importance of the project. [8]

Improve

Now that you have measured and documented the defects of your process, it's time to develop ways to improve it. Once you have a plan for the improvement, it's a good idea to run a pilot test and see if the solution will work as desired.

Have you ever seen leaders make a decision in a vacuum, without truly understanding the process? Unfortunately that's a common mistake even some of the best leaders make. It often goes hand in hand with decisiveness and confidence. I've seen brilliant managers make bad decisions because they didn't take the time to involve the process experts. On the other hand, I've seen mediocre leaders make brilliant decisions by getting the process experts involved.

One way to come up with good ideas to improve a process is by brainstorming. When brainstorming for ways to improve a process, here are a few guidelines to follow that I've seen many successful leaders use:

- Be accepting of all ideas and encourage everyone involved to provide ideas. This is difficult for some people to swallow. It's easy to give more attention and "talk time" to the senior company leaders. Sometimes the associates that are closest to the process come up with the ideas that catch lightning in a bottle.
- Involve as many process experts as possible, but ensure the number of people involved is manageable. Too many people giving ideas at once can become overwhelming in a hurry.

- Make sure you have a scribe to write all ideas down. It's usually best to write these on a large viewable screen or paper, so everyone can understand and build off of the other participant's ideas.
- If there is a large volume of ideas, it helps to segment them into different categories. Stick with one category and brainstorm solutions solely for that segment until the number of ideas slow down, then switch to the next category.
- If ideas are slow to come at first or if the participants are hesitant to provide input, start with all participants writing down ideas silently. After a few minutes, rotate all the papers so the adjacent person can read the ideas, and then add some of their own. Keep rotating the pages until you get a sufficient number of ideas. This often is a good icebreaker before verbally throwing ideas out.
- Last but not least, don't make the brainstorming exercise a "check the block" item as a token gesture to the lower level associates. I've seen very intelligent senior leaders spend hours going through this process, gathering all the information from the participants. After the session was over and the lower level associates had left, they threw out all their ideas and started over with only ideas from the higher management. This is a recipe for disaster. The employees will eventually find out if you try something like this. This is not only a waste of everyone's time, but also a sure way to undermine trust between management and employees. [9]

Another great way to generate solutions in the improve phase is to leverage best practices. Often referred to as process benchmarking, this is simply the process of leveraging the best ways of conducting business from another company or group and utilizing it for your own benefit. Why reinvent the wheel when you can mimic or build upon the great ides of those who have been through this situation before? Keep in mind that utilizing best practices isn't restricted to duplicating a process exactly and plugging it onto the exact same system in another company. For example, a surgical process improvement team looked for ways to decrease their turnaround time for their operating room. They leveraged their improvement ideas from the pit crew of a racing team!

I can't stress enough about how Jack Welch got his managers at GE excited about best practicing. Jack talked about going to Wal-Mart to best practice with their company. This is an interesting point because many would ask, "What does Wal-Mart have to do with GE's business?" It's not like GE is selling toothpaste and baby diapers. Although GE did not directly compete in retail sales with Wal-Mart, there were many common threads between the two companies. As an example, Wal-Mart excelled in the shipping and distribution areas and they offered a wealth of ideas to a company like GE. Getting point of sale data back through the logistics channels quickly, product placement for the customer, and the timing of getting products to market were all ideas that could be shared across a variety of business platforms, no matter what industry they may be servicing.

GE constantly leveraged best practices with external companies as well as its internal companies. As a Black Belt, I personally shared best practices with Bank of America, Northern Trust Bank, PNC Bank, Lexmark, and a variety of companies within GE. As an operations manager I used to hold weekly conference calls with some of my employees in India. We were constantly trying to leverage each other's ideas to improve productivity. There are great ideas all around us out there. All you have to do is just go out and find them!

Finally, in the improve phase you want to test and justify your solutions, then conclude with a cost benefit analysis. Before any major improvement plan is rolled out, it is critical to roll out a pilot of the solution. The pilot solution should be tested on a small group and it should be watched carefully to see if the solution pans out as desired. The idea of utilizing a pilot is to minimize any damage the new process may cause. If the improved process turns out to fail, it will only affect the small pilot group. If necessary, you can make adjustments to the improved process, and test it again using another pilot test. The goal is to verify the pilot works.

A final note on the improve phase is this: in any business you have roadblocks. The roadblocks I'm speaking about now are the other managers or key employees that will resist change and the new process. Their reasons may range from politically motivated ones to fear of change and the unknown. My experience has been it's always easier to include some or all of the people who can be key roadblocks in the Six Sigma project. More than likely, they will resist giving a lot of time and committing to the entire project; however, I find that they usually will take some time to be involved in the improve phase. This gives them an opportunity to dedicate minimal time to the project, yet they can claim to be part of the "fix" to the problem. It's a win – win situation. You eliminate a roadblock by including them in the process and can possibly turn a roadblock into an advocate for your project. This also helps build political bridges between you and the person resisting change. Finally, you get another key member's advice on developing a solution.

Control

The control phase involves the roll-out of the new process, developing an ongoing plan to monitor the new process, and communicating the new process throughout the organization.

Once the pilot is verified and approved, implement the new process in a controlled roll-out across the company. The idea is to minimize potential damages by phasing in the new process using a controlled roll-out across departments and closely monitoring the integration of the new process. Now that you have a new process in place, you should take the time to monitor it. That means metrics! The run chart discussed previously is a common way to monitor defects over time. No matter how you monitor it, the bottom line is if it's important enough to develop a process improvement plan and go through this entire DMAIC process, it warrants the time to measure the new process and ensure it's performing as expected.

Simultaneously, you will need to be an advocate and champion for the new process. You need to communicate the new process to everyone affected and ensure they utilize the "new way of doing business." I've seen project teams do a great job with the first four portions of the DMAIC process, only to fall short at the end and not follow through on communicating the change to the organization. This ultimately leads to people not understanding the new process, not adopting the new process, or worst of all, never even hearing about it. The typical excuse I hear from team members is, "We spent so much time on the project, now we're behind on our *real* work and just don't have the time to do things like a communication plan." You can come up with the greatest idea on the planet, but if you can't communicate it to the right people, nobody will ever know about it.

The Six Sigma DMAIC process can be a very powerful tool. The thing I love about it is the fact that it can work for almost any process and any size business. Keep in mind that what I have presented is a *very* scaled down version of the DMAIC process. I'm not trying to condense the DMAIC methodology, which is typically taught with manuals 600+ pages thick, down into a few paragraphs. I'm simply showing some of the more basic tools that have been utilized by corporations ranging from mom and pop size to larger corporations like 3M, Sears, Merrill Lynch, Lockheed Martin, and Xerox.

PART III
Investing in Real Estate

Markets will change. That is a fact. A tactic used in 2010 may not work in 2020. My intention is to provide you with tactics that many wealthy businesspeople have used over the years to successfully build wealth in the real estate market. This list is not all-encompassing, but rather a list of the popular tactics used by millionaire real estate investors I have known.

In this section I use the term "property" to represent both commercial and residential properties. Most of the tactics discussed in this section are interchangeable between both commercial and residential properties. I've run across so many investors that will stick to only one type of investment. I can understand an investment company not wanting to take on new business if it specializes in one particular type of property and it has all the business it can handle. Sticking to what they know may be the best option for a company in this situation. However, I frequently meet investors that have the time and ability to bring in more projects, but they only look at residential real estate because commercial property scares them. Likewise, I also meet commercial investors that think residential properties are beneath them. This is unfortunate because they are both missing out on opportunities to make money! If you happen to fall into either of these categories, my advice is to expand your horizons. If you have the time and ability, don't let something like a label intimidate you and cause you to lose out on an opportunity!

Why Real Estate Over Stocks?

I get questions like this all the time. People say, "Why should I invest in real estate that is projected to appreciate at a 3% return versus investing in a stock that's showing a consistent 5% return?" First of all, nothing is guaranteed. Nobody can guarantee that stock or mutual fund will even have a positive return. Projected returns on real estate deals are just that – projected. However, real estate investors understand a basic principle that applies across the spectrum of investing, and that is other people's money (OPM). The real estate investor leverages the lender's money to her advantage. This enables her to attain larger returns with less risk. Say we have two investors who each have $20,000 to invest. Investor A puts his money in the stock market while Investor B puts her money into real estate. Investor A puts $20,000 in the stock market and after 5 years he sells and gets a nice return of 5% annually (interest compounded annually) or $5,526 as gross profit. The real estate investment during the same time period does not appreciate as quickly; let's say 3% annually (interest compounded annually). However, Investor B leveraged other people's money to make her investment. She put the $20,000 down to help purchase a $200,000 property. For simplicity's sake, let's assume the rent earned by investor B is exactly enough to cover her $180,000 mortgage payments (interest only), insurance, taxes and closing costs. After two years she sells and the gross profit is $31,855. Investor B had a lower percent return, but she leveraged other people's money to her advantage and earned significantly more interest than Investor A.

Investor A			Investor B	
Initial Investment	$20,000		Initial Investment	$20,000
Value of Investment	$20,000		Value of Investment	$200,000
Annual Return	5%		Annual Return	3%
Gross Profit	$25,526		Gross Profit	$231,855
- Initial Investment	$20,000		- Initial Investment	$ 20,000
			- Mortgage Payoff	$180,000
Net Profit	$ 5,526		Net Profit	$ 31,855

Due to the recession, some might say that their local market won't even support a 3% appreciation rate. Alright, let's look at another example. Here is an apartment complex with 100 units. Operating expenses (vacancy factor, maintenance, management, etc.) are 45% of gross income. The property is appraised at $3,000,000 with $500,000 allocated to the land and $2.5 million as the building's basis for depreciation (@ 3.636%). An investor in the 35% tax bracket may purchase this property with a $500,000 cash down payment to a new $2.5 million first mortgage payable at 8% interest-only, with a balloon payment due in 15 years. Rents range from $250/mo for efficiencies to $650/mo for three bedroom units. The total gross annual rents are $552,000 and there is additional revenue (laundry, vending, parking, etc.) of $13,000. Here is the first year's financial analysis.

Gross Annual Rent	$552,000
Annual Additional Revenue	$ 13,000
Gross Annual Income	$565,000
- Operating Expenses (45%)	$254,250
Net Operating Income	$310,750
- Debt Service ($2.5MM @ 8%)	$200,000
Net Cash Flow	$110,750
- Depreciation ($2.5MM @ 3.636%)	$ 90,900
Taxable Income	$ 19,850
Taxes (35%)	$ 6,948
Net Cash Flow Before Taxes	$110,750
- Taxes	$ 6,948
Net Cash Flow After Taxes	$103,802

Net Cash Flow After Tax / Investment = ROI
$103,802 / $500,000 = 21% Return On Investment

Let's look at the potential stock market return for the same investment.

Initial Investment	$500,000
Value of Investment	$500,000
Annual Return	5%
Gross Profit	$525,000
- Initial Investment	$500,000
Net Profit	$ 25,000

The 21% ROI is looking pretty attractive at this point. This is the way successful investors look at projects. Of course there is a lot more work involved with a owning an apartment complex than owning stocks and mutual funds, even if you have a management staff running the complex. The real value of owning real estate is the power of leveraging other people's money.[11]

Choosing the Right Agent

An agent is someone who acts on another's behalf. Whether you're buying stocks, bonds, mutual funds, a business, building or home, make sure you have the right agent for the job. The agent can be a stock broker, Realtor, friend or family member. Make sure your agent is professional, honest, and has a strong working knowledge of the industry. A good agent can make or break your fortune.

In the real estate market I have seen superb agents work hard for their clients and assist them with finding the best possible deal. In turn, they gain the client's trust and receive repeat business or strong referrals. The right Realtor can help you avoid lawsuits, find investment properties with great value, help you sell your property for the highest possible net return to you, and a myriad of other tasks to include marketing, sales, and research. The single largest financial transaction most people make is the purchase or sale of their home. Make sure you can absolutely trust the people you choose to represent you. Don't judge the book by its cover. Don't choose an agent solely because they have the best looking advertisements or because they have a lot of wealth. You never know how they accumulated the wealth. One example that comes to mind is a pair of real estate agents contracted to sell a piece of property in Florida. The owners lived out of state and trusted them to act in their best interest. After all, the agent only gets paid if they sell the property and the higher the sale price the higher the agent's commission. Sellers generally think with these guidelines the agents are incented to act in the best interest of the seller. Wrong. It doesn't matter how knowledgeable or successful your agents are if they are unethical. These particular agents pushed away potential buyers of the property and discouraged buyers from making offers, thus creating an artificially low market. From the seller's perspective the property wasn't worth as much as their asking price. In fact, the asking price was spot on. The listing agents eventually made their own offer to the sellers; of course it was $80,000 or $90,000 below the true market value. The distressed sellers sold and the agents were able to flip the property for a profit upwards of $80,000.

I've been guilty myself of allowing poor agents to represent me. When I was working on the leadership team with GE in Iowa and spending my evenings and weekends working on my MBA, I had little time to devote to my out of state rental properties. I had previously hired a property manager that was honest, professional and ethical. I personally interviewed him, checked referrals, and ultimately was a satisfied customer for years. Unfortunately, he sold the business and I was too busy to follow up on the new owners. They quickly developed and implemented an interesting business plan. They decided to collect all of the rents from several hundred tenants in their portfolio without paying the landlords. They were able to hold off the screaming landlords for a few months, then left the state and bounced a few checks on the way out just for good measure.

I previously mentioned an acquaintance who owns his own sports management firm that represents NFL players. Pessimists ask, "Why should he make millions just because he knows some rich athletes?" The answer is simple. Because he enables each of his clients to make millions! He negotiates contracts with his client's best interests in mind. He finds alternative ways for them to make more money through endorsements and commercials. He's easily worth the money because he's honest, acts professionally and has a strong working knowledge of the industry. Most importantly, he helps them make more money! The bottom line is be very careful about who you choose to represent you. A good agent can make you a fortune and an unethical one can destroy your finances!

Be Innovative - Think Outside of the Box

In the real estate market it is easy to see which players embrace change and innovation. I once met an agent who had been in the real estate sales field for many years. She told me, "I don't do email." I couldn't believe my ears. I thought either she doesn't need to earn an income or her income earning days are numbered. I've seen sellers throw up their arms and give up trying to sell their homes because they only tried one technique. I've seen investors try to purchase a few properties then give up and admit defeat after only a few tries. They had little to no imagination on how to structure the offers. I was walking by a house one day in one of the neighborhoods I market to and spoke with the owner in the front yard. He told me, "I'm giving my house back to the bank." He tried to sell the home, but went with a traditional brokerage firm and only tried one technique to sell the property. His agent marketed the house on the local multiple listing service and hoped for the best. This single decision cost him $400,000 and was the difference between a profitable sale and a foreclosure! He put all his apples in one basket and it did not work for him. If a house is the largest investment an average American makes in her lifetime, why would she only try one technique to sell it? Here are some ways innovative sellers market their residential and commercial property for sale.

Lease Purchase

The lease purchase has two separate components, the lease and the purchase & sale contract. The buyer enters into a lease contract with the seller for a specific time period. The buyer also has a contract with the seller to purchase the property, at a fixed price or a predetermined scale for adjusting the price over time. For example, the price could be $500,000 if sold in June, and $508,000 if sold in December of the same year. The closing date for the actual sale of the property usually occurs at the end of the lease term or sometimes prior to the end of the lease. There are a few risks involved for the seller. The market could go up and the seller could end up letting the property go for a relatively low price. If the market drops dramatically the buyer could walk away and leave the seller with a vacant house in a down market. The seller can mitigate her risk by requiring a non-refundable fee up front from the buyer. The fee is only given back to the buyer if the buyer purchases the property. If the buyer walks away from the deal, she loses the up front fee. When I do lease purchases, I require an up front non-refundable fee of at least 5% of the purchase price. Lease purchases are generally preferred by sellers. A seller knows she has a contract to sell the property and is guaranteed a certain dollar amount if the buyer walks away.

Lease Option

This is very similar in nature to the lease purchase. In this scenario, the buyer actually has the option to purchase the property. The seller and buyer enter into a lease contract. In the contract the buyer has the option to purchase the property at a specified price and time. The price typically goes up incrementally over a timeline for various closing dates. The buyer/tenant is not obligated to purchase the property. The risk for the seller is the inherent uncertainty involved. The seller does not know if the buyer will purchase the property. The seller can mitigate her risk by working in a right of first refusal in the lease which would allow her to sell the property to another buyer. The seller would, however, be required to give the tenant/buyer a specified amount of advance notice. The tenant/buyer would have the first right to purchase the property or let the second buyer purchase it. The lease option is generally more attractive to buyers. It gives them more flexibility and they usually do not have to pay a non-refundable fee up front. I once used a lease option on a commercial strip center. I wanted to purchase the entire strip center and start a new business in one of the spaces. The lease option helped me reduce my risk and see if the business was successful prior to purchasing the entire building.

Rent Back to Developer

Several developers will agree to sell model homes in a community then rent back the homes until the community inventory is depleted. Typically, builders are able to draw more money from their lenders as they sell more of their inventory, so selling a model allows the developer to sell a home (increasing their cash flow) and also benefit from posting it as a sale on their books. An investor can benefit by having a steady tenant in their property and have time to find the next tenant. In an appreciating market, the investor can usually break even on her cash flow and then realize a nice gain after the neighborhood is built out. Another benefit is utilizing the builder's approved lender. This often provides reductions in closing costs of up to 3% of the sales price. The risk is if the market turns into a declining one. Then the investor is stuck with a property that is difficult to sell and losing value over time.

Sale and Leaseback

The term Rent Back to Developer used in the prior paragraph generally refers to residential properties. The term Sale and Leaseback is the common commercial term for renting back to the developer. A large commercial firm may have to put 20% down to obtain a loan for purchasing a site and building a store. Instead of keeping all this money tied up in the property, the company may opt to sell it to an investor. This way they can get 100% of the value back up front, and then lease the store back from the investor. Leases are generally long term and can range up to 99 years. This benefits the company by freeing up more capital (cash) for it to use elsewhere. Although the company is not building up equity in their property by owning it, they are able to deduct the entire amount of lease payments for taxes. This scenario also gives them some favorable financial ratios by not having the mortgage as a liability on the balance sheet. The investors benefit from this scenario by acquiring a steady return on their investment (ROI) and a stable tenant in a long term lease. Insurance companies are known for purchasing real estate of this kind. My father-in-law was approached by insurance companies interested in his US Government building for the exact same reasons – a steady ROI and a stable tenant on a long term lease.

Owner Financing

Some owners have the luxury of owning their property outright. While marketing their property for sale they can cast a wider net and appeal to more buyers by offering owner financing. There are many buyers out there that do not have the proven credit history to obtain a traditional loan from a bank. If the buyer has some damaged credit, the seller can ask for a larger down payment and can ask for a higher interest rate to cover the risk of lending to someone with damaged credit. Sellers offering owner financing often want it repaid in a few years with a balloon payment. For example, a seller could offer a loan on a 30 year amortization schedule, but after year five, the loan will "balloon" and be due in full. It's easy enough to have an attorney draft up a mortgage, so why don't more buyers and sellers opt for owner financing? Some sellers just need the cash immediately and aren't interested in a slow repayment of the loan.

Many people, both buyers and sellers, are just unwilling to take that step outside of the box. They want the traditional loans and leases that mainstream America is using and they want little to no risk. That's what differentiates innovative people from the rest of the pack. The innovators are willing to stretch themselves and their mindset. They are willing to change and adapt to new ideas.

Going Solo

There are many out there who have successfully bought and sold their own real estate without the assistance of an agent, myself included. I always recommend utilizing the services of an agent. As long as you pick the right one, you'll more than recoup the cost of any commission. However, if you decide to purchase or sell real estate on your own, here are some pointers.

Legal Issues

This is the number one concern I relay to individuals looking to purchase or sell their own property or business. Here are a few of the questions I bring up.

Do you have a contract that will hold up in court? People sometimes have a copy of a contract used from another state. Each state regulates its own real estate industry, so make sure yours is acceptable for the state the property is located in.

How will you handle the escrow money and any disputes over it if the deal goes bad? Ensure you have at least a title company that is handling the binder deposit and language in the contract that specifically discusses any binder disputes.

What real estate attorney are you utilizing? I prefer real estate attorneys to handle closings in case some documentation needs to be drafted at the last minute. I've been in a few situations where the seller required we go through a title company where a paralegal sat in place of the attorney. Paralegals can be great, but inevitably problems arise that attorneys are better suited for. Buyers and sellers should have their own real estate attorneys review all documents prior to signing.

What if the deal doesn't go through? What is your plan of action? Deals frequently do not close due to the actions of the buyer or seller. First of all, since you are solo on this you are responsible for keeping up with all the contractual requirements such as home inspections, wood destroying organism (WDO) inspections, financing requirements, etc. You need to ensure you have met all timeline requirements on your part so you are not in default of the contract. If you are in default, you risk loosing the binder or worse. I've had two experiences where sellers decided at the last minute I (as a buyer) was getting too good of a deal and choose not to sell me the real estate. As the buyer, I needed to ensure I fulfilled all of my requirements outlined in the contract. As long as I fulfilled all of my contractual obligations, I was going to get the property one way or another. Sometimes it takes additional time or money to file a suit against the sellers for breach of contract, but that was my choice to make. On one deal the mere mention of a lawsuit was enough to entice the sellers into going through with the sale. The other was a commercial deal where a company was selling a strip center and some associated machinery on site. The seller decided to ignore the price in the contract and increase the purchase price by roughly

30%. I filed suit and ended up getting a settlement out of court. Between the negative publicity I caused and the loss of money the company incurred, the company I filed suit against had to shut its doors for business. The point is you don't want to be on the wrong end of the lawsuit. Make sure you pay attention to EVERY detail on the contract and be able to DOCUMENT how you fulfilled each of your legal requirements.

How to Prep a Property for Sale

If you are intent on selling your property yourself, here are some quick hints on how to squeeze as much profit out of your property as possible by doing all the *essentials,* yet expending as little cash as possible.

<u>General Guidelines</u>
- This is not the time to remodel, re-landscape and repaint the entire property. Do the projects that will pay off more than the associated investment required. Remodel only if the benefit outweighs the cost.
- Clean and de-clutter the property. Cleaning is imperative inside and out. If the buyers are thinking about how dirty your property is, then they are distracted from the primary focus, which is thinking about occupying the property. If it's residential, they should be thinking about living in it and thinking of where to place their furniture. If it's commercial, they should be thinking about how they are going to build out the property and how they are going to floor plan the space. De-cluttering goes hand in hand with this. A cluttered property distracts buyers and makes it difficult to imagine their furnishings and belongings in the property.
- Look at your property from the customer's prospective. Drive up; walk to the entrance and through the property as if you are the customer. How do the adjacent properties

look? How is the curb appeal? Is it a light and bright appearance or dark and gloomy? Are there any obstacles in your path as you walk inside and out? If so, remove them.

- Ask a friend to walk through the property and note any problems she views. Has a home/building inspection been done recently (i.e. when you purchased)? If not, it's a good idea to have an inspector come through and conduct a full inspection. Correct any major deficiencies prior to putting the property on the market. This places the property in a good light from the buyer's perspective.
- Is it a commercial building we're talking about, perhaps with a business that's being conveyed also? Cash is king and cash flow is absolutely critical. Are you keeping two sets of books – one for the IRS and one for you? I've looked at numerous commercial businesses over the years and I always get a kick out of the seller that states: "Here are my financial statements," then hand me a separate set of books and continues "but these are the ones I give to the IRS." I can't tell you how many times I've heard that line. So, in other words, they're saying I'll lie to the government, but I won't lie to you. Yeah, right. If you want anyone to believe your financials, they better match up with what you report to the IRS for a period of at least three years.

Exterior

- Clean the exterior! I can't emphasize this enough. It is relatively inexpensive to clean and it pays big dividends.
- Ensure the landscaping is up to par. Don't go overboard, but healthy plants, trimmed trees and bushes, and colorful flowers really boost the curb appeal. Keep the landscaping in good shape through mowing and edging. Keep the lawn green as well. This applies to absentee owners also!

- Keep bushes along the walkways trimmed – again, no obstacles blocking the path that buyers will walk.
- Repaint where appropriate. Repainting trim usually makes a dramatic difference for the amount of time and effort required.
- Replace screens, screen doors and windows that are ripped, broken or non-functional.
- Clean windows to allow sunlight in. Ensure lights are functional and provide adequate exterior lighting. Remember, this is not the time to upgrade to your favorite accent lighting package or to replace inefficient high wattage bulbs with eco-friendly ones. Ensure they light the appropriate areas and move on.

Interior

- Clean and de-clutter! Any surprise here? The bathrooms and kitchens should be sanitary and impeccable. No buyer wants to look at a dirty bathroom or kitchen. Again, the buyers want to imagine their belongings in the property. It's hard to do this with your clutter everywhere. If possible pack up as much decorations and clutter as possible and store it off site at an office, relative's house or mini-storage. Closets and rooms look larger if the clutter is removed.
- Eliminate the source of odors and mask any lingering odors. The source can be a number of things: dirty laundry, smoke (cigarette, cigar, pipe), carpet saturated with pet urine, etc. Do as much as you can within reason to remove the source. Have stained carpets or furniture professionally cleaned. Smoke only outside, and board your pet with friends or relatives. Once the source of the odor is removed, continue to air out the home and use odor eliminators and air fresheners as appropriate.
- The pet issue can get touchy with some sellers. Americans love their pets. They usually consider them part of the family. I can assure you that the majority of

residential buyers can tell if a seller has an indoor pet within the first 30 seconds on entering the house. I have never met a pet that helped sell a house. The biggest culprits are dogs. A common occurrence is a dog jumping all over a potential buyer, slobbering on her shoes, and snagging her silk shirt. In this case the buyer leaves with a negative impression of the viewing. Another common occurrence is a really cute dog that steals the show. It may do tricks or wag its tail, all to the adornment of the potential buyer. The problem is that it steals the show away from the property. The customers are distracted from focusing on the property. At a minimum have the pets out of sight during showings. If possible, have them take a pet vacation at the relative's house.

- Inspect your walls, floors and ceiling. Just as with the exterior, repaint where appropriate, and clean the walls and floors. Customers spend a lot of time looking down at the flooring. Repair only the sections of flooring that require it. Wood floors should be polished and carpet should be steam cleaned or chemically cleaned. If repainting a room is required, ensure it's a popular neutral color. You want the colors to be generic and updated so they will appeal to a wide spectrum of buyers versus having outdated or taste specific colors that will only appeal to a small segment of buyers. Again, repainting trim can make a dramatic difference.

2009-10 National Averages [12]

Project	Job Cost	Resale Value	Cost Recouped	Change vs. 2008-09
Attic Bedroom	$49,346	$40,992	83.1%	⬆
Backup Power Generator	$14,304	$8,428	58.9%	⬆
Basement Remodel	$62,067	$46,825	75.4%	⬆
Bathroom Addition	$39,046	$23,233	59.5%	⬇
Bathroom Remodel	$16,142	$11,454	71.0%	⬇
Deck Addition (composite)	$15,373	$10,904	70.9%	⬇
Deck Addition (wood)	$10,634	$8,573	80.6%	⬇
Entry Door Replacement (fiberglass)	$3,490	$2,275	65.2%	⬆
Entry Door Replacement (steel)	$1,172	$1,470	128.9%	⬆
Family Room Addition	$82,756	$54,051	65.3%	⬇
Garage Addition	$58,432	$36,361	62.2%	⬇
Home Office Remodel	$28,375	$13,648	48.1%	⬇
Major Kitchen Remodel	$57,215	$41,260	72.1%	⬇
Master Suite Addition	$103,696	$67,578	65.2%	⬇

Project	Job Cost	Resale Value	Cost Recouped	Change vs. 2008-09
Minor Kitchen Remodel	$21,411	$16,773	78.3%	⬇
Roofing Replacement	$19,731	$13,133	66.6%	⬆
Siding Replacement (vinyl)	$10,607	$8,476	79.9%	⬇
Sunroom Addition	$73,167	$37,118	50.7%	⬇
Two-Story Addition	$156,309	$107,286	68.6%	⬇
Window Replacement (vinyl)	$10,728	$8,217	76.6%	⬇
Window Replacement (wood)	$11,700	$9,044	77.3%	⬇

Be Situationally Aware of the Market and Understand Which Repairs/Remodels are Appropriate

How many times have you heard of sellers claim "I sold my house by remodeling my floors, kitchens, bedroom, etc. and sold it for $50,000 more than I initially paid for it"? That's great, but what if the remodel job cost $60,000? I see both sides of this scenario frequently. I know people who are adept at valuing property, purchasing it and adding just the right touches to get it to sell at a profit. I also hear horror stories from those who made the wrong decisions on the remodeling and came up short at closing. Full remodel jobs can be great if the situation warrants it. For example, say you find a foreclosure in a neighborhood where similar sized homes are selling for $500,000. All of the appliances have been removed by the previous owners on their way out, the flooring is worn and needs to be replaced throughout the house, the counters were badly damaged by the unprofessional removal of the appliances, and graffiti was spray painted throughout the interior walls. You're able to negotiate a price of $400,000. It takes $30,000 to paint and install flooring, counters, and appliances comparable to that found in other homes in the neighborhood. Now you've got a home valued at $500,000 and only paid $430,000 for it, giving you $70,000 in instant equity. In this situation it is appropriate to do some remodeling.

Let's look at another example where an investor picks up a distressed sale that has a water leak and mold in one of the interior walls in a guest bedroom. It also has some worn carpeting in the main living area and cracked tiles in the kitchen. Other than those three problems the house is in great shape and shows very well. The investor is able to get the property for $120,000. Similar sized properties in the neighborhood are selling for $180,000. He finds out the mold remediation will cost $6,000. He asks some neighbors and finds out that the majority of homes in the neighborhood have lower grade ceramic tile in the kitchens and carpet in the living areas, just like the flooring in his property. He gets a quote of $4,000 for new tile and carpet that would be comparable to the flooring found in other homes in the neighborhood. If he follows this course of action he theoretically has a property worth $180,000 and only $130,000 in it, giving him $50,000 in equity. This would be an appropriate course of action for the investor. Instead of following this course of action, let's say he decides to take the opportunity to upgrade the flooring by installing cherry wood in the living area and slate in the kitchen, in the hopes of boosting the property's value even higher. Now he has the cost of the property at $120,000, the mold remediation cost of $6,000 and a cost of $12,000 for the upgraded slate and wood flooring. How much value will he get out of adding the upgraded slate and wood flooring? I get questions like this all the time. Will he get *more* than the $12,000 back that he invested in the upgraded flooring? Or better yet, will he even break even on the $12,000 investment? The answer is *No*, at least not in this instance. Why? Because he over-invested in the project. Nothing against slate and cherry wood floors, but the return is not going to justify the investment in this situation. Typically, buyers are going to pay a certain price range for a certain neighborhood, no matter how much money a seller has invested in a home. As an extreme example say you have two neighborhoods. One has homes that sell for $400,000 - $600,000 and the other has much larger and opulent homes that range from $800,000 – $1,000,000. If you could move one of the homes valued at $900,000 from the higher priced area and move it to a lot in the lower priced area, no buyer would pay $900,000 for the home in the lower priced area. The surrounding homes would bring the house value down. A more prestigious neighborhood also carries a brand value that adds to the value of the home. The same holds true for over-investing in an existing home. You can do as much remodeling as your bank account will allow, but once you start to exceed the existing standards in the neighborhood, you will see diminishing returns on your invested dollars.

I use the term "situationally aware" of the market because each circumstance in real estate is unique. No two properties occupy the same space. Whether they are differentiated by location, view, size, age, condition or zoning, they each are unique in some way. I *frequently* get questions about how various remodel jobs will affect property values. During the time of writing *this paragraph* I received a call from a client asking about adding a guest bathroom and how it would affect the sale price of their home. When people ask about remodeling a home, the return on the amount of money invested in the remodel really depends on the situation. For example, say you live in a house that has no flattering views of the surrounding area. Adding a widow's walk on top of a house that provides you with a better view of your neighbor's back yard is generally useless. However, if your neighbor's yard is next to the ocean and you now have gained a scenic ocean view; your property value may have gone up triple the amount of the cost of the deck. Let's look at another example of a house with four bedrooms and two baths. The owner wants to add another bedroom and hopes to recoup more than the $20,000 required for the addition. Other homes in the neighborhood tend to have from three to four bedrooms. In this situation, it is not prudent to add another bedroom. If he had a two bedroom home in the same neighborhood it would probably make economic sense to add the extra bedroom.

The same can be said for under-investing. For example, say an investor is flipping a house in a neighborhood with similar homes valued at $800,000. The previous owner had a fire and the home has significant smoke damage. The investor is able to get it for a good price, but has to do extensive work inside. The majority of the homes in the area have marble or travertine flooring, granite or quartz counters and custom cabinetry. The investor decides to remodel everything, but wants to maximize his profit by keeping his expenses down. He decides to use lower grade products like carpet instead of marble, laminate counters instead of solid surface, and lower quality cabinetry. He has now under-invested in the property. Buyers in this particular market are not looking for a low grade product. Buyers more than likely will rip apart the investor's remodel work and have their own upgraded remodeling done which better blends with the neighborhood. This blunder on the investor's part will cost him time on the market (weeks or months that the house will sit vacant without selling) because it is undesirable and it will produce a lower sales price due to the undesirable remodeling package he chose.

Over-investing and under-investing can lead to a lower return on your investment. Be careful and remain situationally aware of what buyers and sellers are doing in the local market. You may have heard the phrase "Choose the right tool for the job." Choosing the right remodel for the property can pay big dividends on the bottom line and assist in getting the property sold as quickly as possible.

Searching For Property

Searching for real estate on your own can be time consuming and tedious, but it can pay off when you find that gem. The right agent can have a vast array of resources to find good deals. If you don't have that agent that is willing or capable of assisting you, here are some tips.

Get out there and learn the market. Pick a target area and start driving the streets. Before you can understand the value of a good or service, you must first understand the product. Make it part of your daily or weekly routine to look for real estate. Many of the deals out there are not the traditional sales marketed by real estate brokers. Look for the FSBO (For Sale By Owner) properties. I've seen plenty of homes for sale by owner that were not priced correctly. On occasion I've seen homeowners that chose not to go through a professional agent to list their property and listed the property too low due to not having updated and accurate pricing information. Keep an ear open for the properties not on the market yet. Divorce, death, bankruptcy and other life changing events create opportunity for those who are ready, willing and quick to make an offer. If you are tuned in to a neighborhood and know who is going through life changing events, opportunity is knocking. The question is, are you going to open the door? Many people are too embarrassed or fearful to approach a person in financial distress. They don't want to seem like vultures. The truth is your offer to buy their property at a discounted rate may be just what they need. As long as the offer is made with tact and respect, it can be the answer to their prayers.

When I was in asset management with GE, I handled some repossessions of our customer's inventory. Usually this was due to a bankruptcy. I always held an initial briefing for the logistics company handling the transportation and disposition of the equipment. I would explain the situation to them and request they be respectful toward the owners as they haul off the last bits of inventory and forever close the doors on their business. More than once I witnessed truck drivers make an offer to the business owners for a refrigerator or stove. The naysayers would cringe at this and utter words like "vulture." In truth, this was a win-win situation for all involved. As long as the negotiated price was higher than the wholesale value GE required for the equipment, the owner made a small profit along with GE. It was also one less piece of equipment GE would have to transport to a holding facility, store, and transport again to an auction company or another appliance dealer. The truck drivers would get a significant discount and everyone was happy! The opportunists who identified a situation for a great deal used tact and wound up winners! They let the naysayers go along with the other sheep who pay full price for appliances.

What to Look For

"Be fearful when others are greedy and greedy only when others are fearful." – Warren Buffett

There is a tremendous amount of opportunity out there in real estate. The single largest investment most people make is purchasing their primary residence. In turn, distressed sales can be a tremendous opportunity for investment. Where do you start looking for deals? In the ocean of real estate for sale one can easily swim in circles until they are disoriented and sinking to the bottom, feeling only frustration and anxiety as they grasp for the right answers. My best advice; develop a plan and stick with it. Your plan can be flexible and understand that changes will need to be made, but don't keep making wholesale alterations to your strategy. Don't jump from strategy to strategy without giving each the time to develop to fruition.

A Note on Flipping

I will cover several different tactics to use for acquiring real estate below market value. Once an investor has acquired the property, it's up to that investor to decide which course of action is best – selling or leasing. He must judge the risk involved, current market conditions for renting and selling, costs for repairs, etc. He must also take into consideration his strengths and weaknesses. Is the investor adept at selling property, or is he better suited for leasing? What are the long term goals of the investor? Is he looking for a steady stream of cash flow over several years as a landlord or a quick return in a lump sum as a seller? Flipping was a very common technique between the years of 1994 – 2006. These investors were fortunate to operate during this gold rush. The ensuing real estate crash was generally devastating, with some areas adversely affected more than others. Parts of California, Florida, Nevada and Arizona were absolutely crushed.

Flippers can no longer rely on quick (or in some instances *any*) price appreciation. So now everyone at the cocktail parties is saying flipping properties is an obsolete technique that will never be used again. Wrong. Flipping may be passé for the majority of those doing it between the years of 1994 – 2006, but for the real investors it's still a viable means of earning a good return on your investment. Even in some of the hardest hit parts of Florida I still see successful investors making strong returns on flipping property. How is this possible? It's really simple. Since they can't rely on price appreciation anymore, they rely on acquiring the property at a price below market value. Here are some strategies to use.

Short Sale

These properties are worth less than what is owed to the lender(s). In other words, the homeowner is upside down, and after the home is sold the lender(s) are looking at a loss based on what is owed to them. Note that often the lenders sell the mortgage to other lenders or investors. Here's a common example of a short sale process. A buyer purchased a house at or near the top of the real estate market when prices were outrageous. The buyer purchased the property with a conventional loan that was interest only and had a 3 year arm. In this scenario, the buyer only pays interest (no principal) on the loan for the first 3 years and the interest rate is at a relatively low fixed rate. After the 3 year period is up, the rate adjusts to the current market or index rate, which could be much higher than the initial lower rate. On top of this, the buyer now has to start paying the principal. This could lead to situations where buyers wind up increasing their monthly mortgage payment by 50% or more! Throw in a declining real estate market and the buyer is stuck with an enormous mortgage payment and a home that's worth much less than what they owe on it. Hundreds of thousands of people have found themselves in this situation and look to the lenders for assistance. The lenders have to authorize the sale of the property since they are going to take a loss on the amount owed to them (known as a write-off).

Each lender has their own thresholds for the amount of write-offs they will take throughout the year. These write-off thresholds may also vary from year to year and quarter to quarter, depending on the economy, the projected earnings of the lender, and various other internal factors. The important thing to understand is the fact that lenders are likely to negotiate and take a loss when a homeowner comes to them with a hardship request and wants to utilize the short sale process. I mention hardship because the lenders will only allow those customers enduring a hardship to utilize the short sale process. Otherwise, the lenders would have all shut their doors years ago due to forgiving billions of dollars of debt! If the property cannot be sold through the short sale process, the next step is foreclosure. The short sale is the lesser of the two evils for the lender. The short sale will typically provide the lender with a smaller loss than the foreclosure and is therefore more appealing. Typically the lender will order a Broker's Price Opinion (BPO – a scaled down version of an appraisal conducted by a real estate professional), an appraisal, or both after they receive an offer on a short sale. These are used to determine the *Market Value* of the house. Once the market value is determined, the lender will *usually* accept a loss based as a percentage of the market value, *not the Amount Owed the Lender*.

As an example, say a buyer purchased a home in 2006 at the height of the real estate boom for 200,000. They financed 100% of the purchase price with a 5% interest only teaser interest rate that adjusted two years later to a 6.75% fixed rate fully amortized loan. If they did not pay any money toward the principal during those two years, their principal + interest mortgage payment went from $833.33/month to $1,297.20/month. This is an increase of 56%! Many homeowners who face these challenges end up in the short sale process.

Keeping with the same example, let's say the house went on the market as a short sale. Assuming the local market dropped 20% during the two year period, the market value in 2008 is $160,000. Many lenders will allow the property to be sold for a percentage of the market value. I've seen some short sales go for as much as 20% below market value. So that house that the buyers purchased in 2006 for $200,000 *could* be sold two years later for as little as $128,000!

Short sales allow a buyer to purchase properties **below market value**. However, as short sales have become more prevalent and lenders have lost more and more money, they have become much more stringent about the short sale process. Lenders and investors are constantly changing the requirements for the short sale process and the thresholds for their write-off allowances.

The short sale process is a slow one. The seller must notify the lender that they wish to conduct a short sale. Most lenders have a standardized packet they send to the seller to fill out. At a minimum the lender will want to see items such as recent bank statements and recent pay stubs. They may request the seller write a letter to explain their hardship or they may request tax returns. Once the lenders have these items, they open a file and wait for a contract. Once a contract is submitted to the lender, the lender will assign a processor. In 2006 this may have taken a few days on average. By 2008 some lenders were taking several months to get a processor assigned. They were so inundated with the amount of short sales on their books that the cycle time, or amount of time that elapsed from receiving an offer to closing on the property, had gone from roughly 45 days in 2006 to 6 months or more in 2008. More recently the lenders have started to adjust to the volume of short sales and are improving the wait time for getting a processor assigned. After the lender has reviewed the file and contract, they may accept it, deny it, or make a counter offer.

One critical rule to understand about short sales is the propensity for taxable gains. When the lender takes a loss, it becomes a gain for the seller. This gain may be taxable by the IRS. So when the seller buys a house for $300,000 with zero down in 2006 then sells it as a short sale for $150,000 in 2010, the $150,000 loss the lender takes is considered a taxable gain. The IRS is making some exclusions for that gain. For example, primary residences have been excluded in the past. If you're selling and considering a short sale, be sure you consult your tax professional first.

A common misconception about short sales is the role the seller has. Most buyers forget about the seller and think the decision making process lies entirely with the lender(s). Wrong. The seller is the one that has the power to initiate the short sale process with the lender. The seller can also choose to end the short sale process. The seller still has to sign off on any contracts prior to the sale of the property. The seller can decide which offers may be submitted to the lender(s). If the seller is looking at a potential taxable gain of $150,000 like in the previous example, you better believe she is going to try her hardest to get the most money she can for her property and reduce that potential gain! Most of the buyer's agents I have dealt with do not understand this concept. They typically get indignant when the seller won't submit their lowball offer to the lender(s). When buying or selling short sales, I strongly recommend utilizing the services of an experienced professional. It can easily save you thousands of dollars.

When it comes to making an offer on a short sale, I suggest making offers on as many properties as possible. A good agent can assist in writing attractive contracts with no binder deposits. The more fishing poles you have in the water, the better your chances of catching that trophy marlin! Don't put all your eggs in one basket. Even if you fall in love with one property, put in as many offers as you can. If you're writing offers with no binder deposits, there is no risk for the buyer. Why not increase you chances of getting a steal by making multiple offers?

Foreclosures

These properties have more than likely already been through the short sale process. The owner of a foreclosure has failed to make the required mortgage payments and the lender has exercised their right of foreclosure. Upon foreclosure, typically the lender will assign the property to their internal REO (Real Estate Owned) department. This internal department will utilize their preferred method of disposing of the property. Remember, the lenders DO NOT want to be landlords. They want to be in the lending business. They want to get rid of these properties as quickly and as efficiently as possible. They are looking at a non-earning asset sitting on their books. Once they have foreclosed on a property, there is no owner for their collections department to call. There is no chance of restructuring the loan with the owner. The house is vacant and they need to dispose of it quickly. These properties will sell much faster than short sales. If they have not already done so, they will have an appraisal or BPO conducted. The lender can dispose of the property by using their own internal process such as advertising it on their company website, or outsource it to a real estate professional, such as an auction company or a real estate broker that will list it.

The great thing about a foreclosure is that the lenders have a solid idea of how much they will accept for the property and can close fairly quickly, usually within 30 days or less. They generally require a binder deposit with a contract, but once an offer is presented they can usually make a quick decision. They will accept the contract, reject the contract, or make a counter offer. In the markets I analyzed, the average LIST price for a foreclosed property was lower than short sale properties. The average SALE price was also lower and the TIME it took to sell the property was significantly lower also. In the areas I looked at, the average List price was **16%** less than short sales in the same market, the average Sale price was **15%** less than short sales in the market, and the average TIME to sell the property was **89%** less than the time to sell short sales in the same market. This goes to prove the point that once lenders become home owners, they do everything they can to get rid of the property. It is for these reasons that foreclosures are *generally* a better deal than short sales. Remember, these are just averages. There are still plenty of great deals in the short sale family out there. You just have to be selective.

Auctions

Auctions are utilized by a variety of individuals and institutions to liquidate assets. The assets can range from toy dolls to oceanfront mansions and everything between. Real estate is auctioned by lenders (typically online), real estate brokers, and auction companies. You can find some great deals paying pennies on the dollar at times but beware; auctioneers are in business for a reason. Many people think that just because they bought it at an auction, it's a great deal. Wrong. Some properties sold at auction go at higher prices than they could command on the traditional market. I was at an auction once that sold approximately 12 townhomes that were almost identical. The variance in price between the first one auctioned and the last one was enormous. The first sold in the high $700,000 range and the last sold in the high $400,000 range. How do you think the first purchasers felt at the end of the auction?

Before you go to an auction, I recommend first asking if the auction is absolute. An absolute auction means the property will be sold to the highest bidder no matter how low the winning bid is. There is no reserve price at a true absolute auction. The reserve price is the price fixed as the minimum at which property will be sold at an auction. The reserve price may or may not be announced at the start of the auction. Beware: occasionally you will find auction companies that advertise an auction as absolute, but announce at the last minute that there is a reserve price. It's also a good idea to ask if there is a minimum bid prior to going to an auction. If there is a minimum bid requirement, it should be disclosed prior to the auction.

My father-in-law started working with auctions initially by working with banks and their properties that were in various stages of default. Once he established a reputation of confidentiality, trust and honesty with the banks and their defaulting clients, his auction business increased and he eventually established a partnership with a reputable auctioneer. Over a ten year period they held many marina, condominium, and bankruptcy auctions. He likes bankruptcy auctions because the sellers need to liquidate the assets. The bankruptcy court assigns the case to a trustee. The trustee is an attorney that needs to liquidate the assets as part of their duty to the court. The trustee typically will hire a real estate broker to sell the property or utilize an auction company to liquidate the assets. Typically the auction will be absolute. My father-in-law once held an absolute auction for a bankruptcy case that involved a fitness center. The facility and its contents were in mint condition and went for pennies on the dollar!

Other Distressed Sales

We've covered short sales, foreclosures, auctions, and bankruptcies. All of these are at some level a distressed sale. Let's take a look at one other segment we haven't mentioned yet. How about the properties that have not yet migrated into the above categories? In many markets I have found that the short sales, foreclosures, auctions and bankruptcies drive the market. That is, they set the price for the low end of the market. Once these properties sell, everyone else in the market must reevaluate their price and possibly drop them. I find plenty of sellers that need to sell their property due to a death in the family, job relocation, job loss or a variety of other reasons. They realize that if they want to sell their property they must compete with the foreclosures, short sales, etc. As a result they price their property competitively with the other distressed sales. These properties can be gems. For example, foreclosures typically are not in good cosmetic condition and often need maintenance or even remodeling, sometimes costing up to tens of thousands of dollars. Prior to going into foreclosure, the typical owner is not happy with the lender or the situation in general and will not maintain the property over the last few months of possession. I've seen several instances where the sellers removed appliances, light fixtures, even air conditioners prior to leaving the property. If you can find a seller that has enough equity in the property that enables him to sell without going through the short sale process and they price the property to sell quickly (i.e. they price it competitively with other distressed sales in the market) then you have a good chance of finding a property that is in good condition and priced well. I've seen multiple investors hone in on properties like these and add them to their portfolios.

Some other distressed sales result from homes that just have problems. There is an array of issues that can plague a home including but not limited to: wood destroying organisms (WDO) such as termites or wood rot, mold, structural problems, water intrusion, cracked slabs, builder defects, fogged windows, boundary disputes, and so on. Not to mention some homes are just plain ugly. Many people treat these homes like a rattle snake. Stay away and do not touch. If the owner does not address the problem or does not address it correctly, the property's value will plummet. There are just some things that scare potential buyers to death. Properties with problems like the ones previously mentioned can be diamonds in the rough. I had an attorney that worked on my sales team. She owned two companies that would market to distressed sellers, purchase their homes, then remodel and rent or sell the property. She loved homes with mold. She knew these would scare most buyers away. Even some of the investors would shy away from homes requiring mold remediation. The savvy investor will look at properties like these and assess the amount of money and effort it will take to remediate the problems. In a way, investors actually have a competitive advantage over people that are buying properties for personal use. Most residential properties are sold and purchased by people who want to live in them. These individuals tend to have a strong emotional attachment to their property. The investor can look objectively at a property and make a cold, calculated financial decision. Most non-investors cannot do this. For instance, many residential buyers want nothing to do with the words termite or mold. They hear them once and run the other way. Investors making a financial decision can evaluate the risk with the reward and make an unemotional financial decision.

How do you find out about these problems? Often they are disclosed up front. Most Realtors are going to have their clients fill out and sign a property disclosure statement. Be careful; just because an owner filled out a property disclosure doesn't mean they're coming clean on all the things that are wrong with the property. That leaky roof may have "slipped their minds" while the owners were filling out the disclosure. So what can you do to reduce your risk? First of all, demand a seller's property disclosure that is signed by the owners. At a minimum, this gives you some legal recourse if you can prove they lied about a blatant defect. People in general also find it a little harder to bend the truth when they are signing their name on a document. The second and probably most important thing you can do to unveil problems with a home is to hire a home inspector (or building inspector for commercial property). A good home inspector is worth his weight in gold to a potential buyer. They can go through the structure and major systems of a home and reveal items such as useful life remaining on a roof, water leakage/intrusion, mold, cracks in walls, and performance of HVAC system. The list goes on. A few hundred dollars up front is well worth the money before any investment, be it thousands or hundreds of thousands. Hand in hand with the home inspector is the WDO inspector, who looks for signs of any previously existing or live wood destroying organisms as well as any damage they have caused. Remember, home inspection companies and WDO inspection companies are like any other business group. There are plenty of good ones and bad ones. Find a winner and stick with it.

The smart investors are objective in their decision making. They look at the big picture. They look at the scope of purchasing, remodeling, and then marketing the property for lease or sale. These acts are linked together in a project. With every project there's management time and expenses that are required. Good investors know how to examine the project in its totality and make valid estimates on the costs and revenue involved in the project. If the project is cost effective, they go through with it.

Validate Your Information

It doesn't matter what you are purchasing: a commercial business, a commercial strip center, a commercial lot, a triplex, a single family home to be used as your primary residence, or anything in between. *You must validate the information you are receiving*! I cannot stress this enough, because I have seen misinformation given out on several occasions. I hate to use the work lie, but I think it's necessary in this case. I have seen real estate brokers, real estate sales agents, property managers, sellers, buyers, lenders, and countless others lie to their customers in order to close a deal. Fortunately this is the exception and not the rule. I have personal experience receiving some bad information and making a financial decision based on that information. I can assure you that it feels like a rotten pit in your gut when you discover that you have been duped. Anyone making any sort of financial investment should double check all the pertinent facts with a credible outside source.

Think of all the variables that can affect the value of your purchase. For residential properties, you want to be sure you cover the basics. Verify the insurance that is required and get quotes from multiple sources. I've seen property insurance quotes for the same property vary as much as 279% between different insurance companies. The A rated insurance company you've always purchased coverage through may be on the high end of the spectrum, while the seller may be giving you an insurance quote from a subpar company on the opposite end of the spectrum. Ask the homeowner's association (HOA) about future plans for fences and streets that border the property as well as any changes to or problems with community centers or other common amenities. Are there problems with owners in the HOA that are delinquent on their dues? I've seen condos in some cities that are only 30% built out. The developers got caught building at the peak of the housing bubble and are paying the HOA fees for 70% of the condos. Some of these condo developers are bleeding $32,000 + each month. You may find a great price on a unit, but how long will the developer keep losing cash until they file for bankruptcy? How about the nature preserve your real estate agent talks about in the back of the property. Is it a protected wetland, or is it merely a wooded area that can be developed in the future? Often the two can look exactly the same. I've seen people pay a premium for a nature preserve view, only to watch in horror as it is stripped bare and their nature view turns to a view of another house. Be sure to investigate with the county. Don't assume zoning is consistent throughout your neighborhood. In Houston I've watched residential homes with wooded views change to homes with views of a parking garage. Again, go to the county and check on the zoning of properties in your vicinity.

Commercial purchases can be a little more challenging at times. Sometimes there is no source of information to validate what you are looking for. What then? You have to get creative. Mr. Moldt preached to his entrepreneurial students the importance of conducting your due diligence prior to purchasing a business. Sometimes you have to get creative and think outside of the box. For instance, a road widening may assist or hinder a commercial business that borders that road. Checking with the DOT or county about any traffic pattern changes or road alterations planned is a good idea prior to purchasing a business located on a public road.

To the small business owner, the single most important financial report is the cash flow statement. If you're looking to buy an existing business, start one yourself, or purchase investment real estate, make sure you have a very clear picture of the cash flow. If buying an existing business, assume the financial records are falsified. The reason is simple; business owners who do not report all of their cash income have a lower tax basis and therefore pay fewer taxes. Make the seller prove to you the validity of the records. Demand federal and state tax returns. If the seller admits that they've been lying to the IRS, then what's to stop them from lying to you? As I previously mentioned, I've had sellers show me the books they report to the IRS, then pull out a separate set of books that reflect the "real" cash flow. This is a catch 22 for the owner, because in the short term they gain a tax advantage but in the long term it's difficult for them to sell a business based off of falsified books. An owner who nets $500,000/yr but only reports $300,000 to the government is going to have a much harder time selling the business for what it's truly worth. If you're a business owner trying to sell, make sure you have at least three years of accurate income statements if you want to get the true value of the business.

Some buyers look at businesses that have been in operation less than a year. Some are interested in a start-up. If you're considering starting up a business or purchasing an existing business that does not have detailed or complete financial records, use some common sense techniques to estimate the revenue potential. In retail operations, watch the store during peak times and slow times. Watch the traffic coming in and out. Take notice of what people are buying and the volume of items purchased. Then it's simple math to make some rough estimates of the gross sales. In service industries it's often easy to look at the input and understand what the output is. I used to own a drycleaner and laundromat business. A quick look at the gas and water bills will give you a good idea of how much business the owners are truly getting. The same goes for a gas station/convenience store. My friend that amassed a large portfolio of convenience stores knows that the volume of gas pumped can give a good indication of what number of customers and inside sales to expect. Ask for a pro-forma cash flow statement (which gives an estimate of future cash flow) and bounce off your findings with what they have. If there is a significant gap, ask questions and do some research. There may be a good explanation or maybe they're just inflating the numbers. If it's a start-up business, request all the information you can from the franchisor (if applicable) and research the competitors in the area. BE CONSERVATIVE! Don't overestimate your revenue or underestimate your expenses!

Know Your Customer

This goes hand in hand with Validate Your Information. I've seen landlords of residential and commercial property get so anxious to lease out a space, they forgo the credit check. Big mistake! Know who you're dealing with. If you're going to be their landlord or if you're structuring an owner financing deal (where the owner lends the buyer all or part of the money required to purchase the property), you are going to have a long-term relationship with this customer. Red flags on a credit or background check can cause a deal to be restructured to provide less risk for you or it can even kill a deal altogether. Evicting tenants or repossessing a car is generally a lose-lose situation. It's better to wait for the right tenants rather than settle for ones that can destroy your property. In the 1980s I watched a movie called Pacific Heights about a tenant who did not pay rent and spent all of his free time demolishing the rental unit. Most of my friends thought this was a good fictional movie, but a little over the top. Unfortunately I have seen this happen to a family member. The tenant ripped out everything that he possibly could. The fans, lights, and electrical outlets were all taken! If a credit or background check comes back with red flags, don't be afraid to ask for more money or collateral up front as security to reduce your risk. Don't get too anxious. Be decisive, but make an informed decision.

GE Capital had the same issues. They would set up rigorous screening guidelines for their customers to go through prior to funding any deals. There were still some companies that would slip through the cracks and manage to defraud GE out of hundreds of thousands of dollars. Even some of the long-term customers with fairly strong payment histories would "lose" hundreds of thousands of dollars of their collateralized inventory before closing their business. In a worst case scenario I had to go to a deposition for one of our customers who had managed to defraud GE out of millions!

Ensure you know your customer before you entrust them with your money or property. When you're anxious about losing a customer to the competition, it's painful to wait for that credit report or list of references. Trust me, it's even more painful to go back and evict a tenant or repossess collateral. And it's even more painful still to go back and attempt an eviction or repossession only to find out the property has been destroyed or stolen!

Not Enough Time?

Managing a real estate investment, whether it is investing in commercial property, investing in residential rentals, or purchasing a business, will require some time on your part. The time requirement obviously corresponds with the type and size of investment, but even if you have another party managing your investment you will likely dedicate some of your time overseeing things. If you don't have the time to dedicate or the appetite for the risk involved, investing in a REIT, or real estate investment trust, may be best for you. The REIT resembles a mutual fund in some ways. A mutual fund pools money and invests it into a variety of stocks, bonds, and other securities. Remember how diversification reduces the risk of the investment? REITs are similar in that they invest in a variety of real estate, thus utilizing diversification to reduce risk. REITs are required to distribute the majority of their income back to the shareholders, a feature that is attractive to many investors. You can go through a brokerage firm or wealth manager to invest in REITs. Another advantage of REITs is their liquidity. They are much more liquid than traditional real estate investments. Selling shares of a REIT is much easier and quicker than selling a building, and selling a share of a REIT quickly should result in little loss of value. The downside of investing in a REIT is you don't have direct control over the trust and a portion of the money invested goes toward the costs associated with a professional management staff running the operation. So if you're looking for a real estate investment that doesn't require the time and effort required in the day to day management of a traditional real estate investment with a relatively lower amount of risk and more liquidity, the REIT may be for you.

If you do have the time and resources to invest in real estate, it can be very rewarding on many different levels. Building your own business from the ground up gives a sense of pride, confidence and satisfaction that is unrivaled. One of the best projects I have been involved with was building a business in the roughest part of town. I took a building that was nothing more than a burnt out shell and turned it into a thriving strip center. I created jobs, I met a lot of wonderful people, I helped beautify a former eyesore, and I made some money in the process!

Final Thoughts

I will echo some advice given to me by Ed Moldt. In the late 1980s he joined the Wharton School of Business and was managing director of their entrepreneurial center. [13] While there, he would tell his students to start their own business as quickly as possible. He did not want them to wait until they graduated. He advised them to start something immediately, no matter how small it was! The toughest part is getting past that initial inertia. Once you've started one, the next will be much easier on your emotions! So get out there and start!

Reference List

1 http://chriscunard.com/queen_elizabeth1.php

2 Daytona Beach Morning Journal, Daytona Beach, FL
September 7, 1970

Gordon R. Ghareeb,
http://www.maritimematters.com/elizabeth-ghareeb.html
2005

3 Philip Morris 1967 Annual Report,
http://tobaccodocuments.org/ti/TIMN0439886-
9925.html?zoom=750&ocr_position=above_foramatted&
start_page=1&end_page=40

4 http://www.microsoft.com/Presspass/press/2009/jan09/01-
07VerizonSearchPR.mspx Jan. 7, 2009

5 Mark Clothier, Best Buy Plan to Take on Verizon May
Boost Earnings (Update1),
http://www.bloomberg.com/apps/news?pid=20670001&si
d=adeUksWmTU7o, June 4, 2007

6 Michael Brassard & Diane Ritter, GE Capital Services
Memory Jogger™ II, GOAL/QPC, 1994

7 Ibid

8 Ibid

9 Ibid

10 Wikipedia,
http://en.wikipedia.org/wiki/List_of_Six_Sigma_compani
es, Feb. 26, 2010

142

11   Cooke Real Estate School Florida Essentials of Real
      Estate Investment: 30-Hour Broker Post-Licensing
      Course, Version 3.0

12   Remodeling Cost vs. Value Report 2009-2010,
      Remodeling Magazine,
      http://www.remodeling.hw.net/2009/costvsvalue/national.
      aspx, 2010

12   George McCrory, Three New Companies Join UI
      Technology Innovation Center, The University of Iowa
      News Services, http://www.news-
      releases.uiowa.edu/2000/march/0317tech_tenants.html,
      March 17, 2000

www.ingramcontent.com/pod-product-compliance
Lightning Source LLC
Chambersburg PA
CBHW051531170526
45165CB00002B/692